# AFRICAN SAFARI

## INTO THE GREAT GAME RESERVES

— PETER & BEVERLY PICKFORD —

- PETER & BEVERLY PICKFORD -

# AFRICAN SAFARI

## INTO THE GREAT GAME RESERVES

jb

JOHN BEAUFOY PUBLISHING

# DEDICATION

This book is dedicated to those who have in some way tied their life's work to the conservation and awareness of African wilderness, and amongst whom we had the privilege to work.

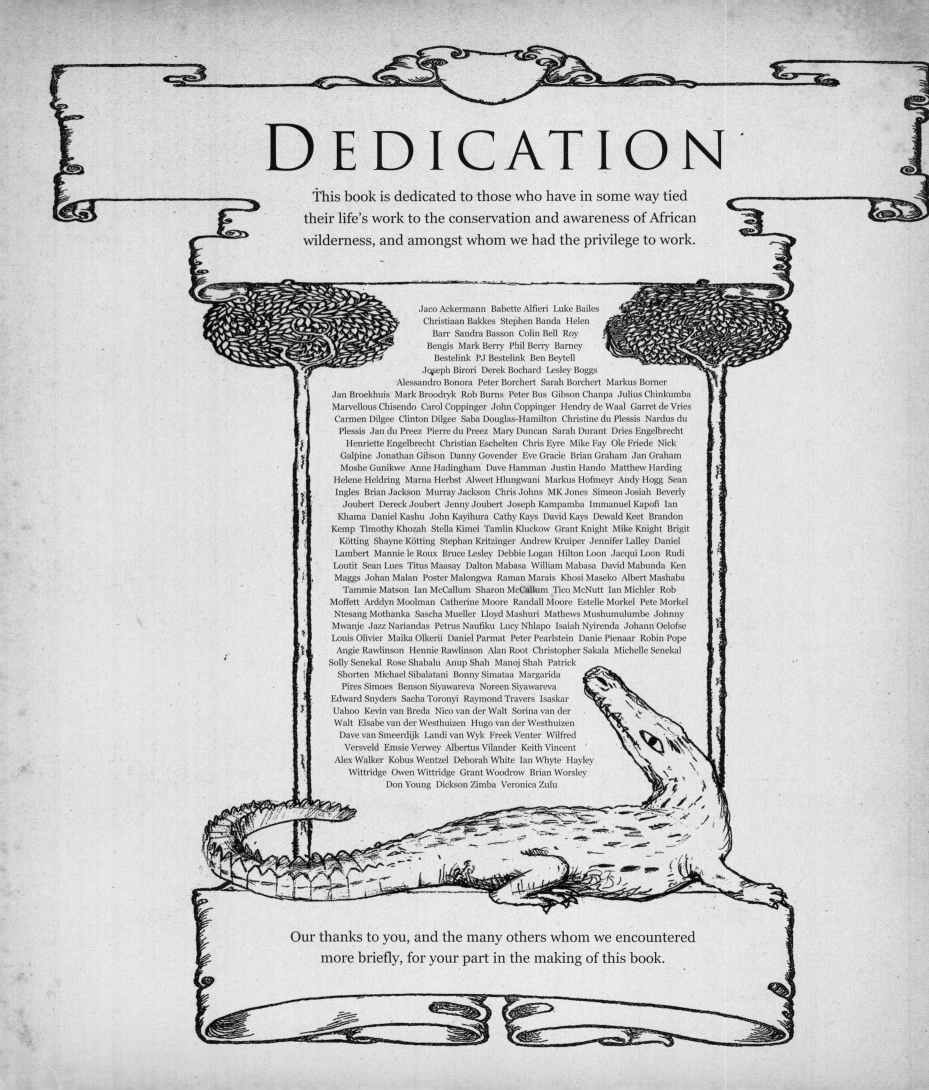

Jaco Ackermann  Babette Alfieri  Luke Bailes  Christiaan Bakkes  Stephen Banda  Helen Barr  Sandra Basson  Colin Bell  Roy Bengis  Mark Berry  Phil Berry  Barney Bestelink  PJ Bestelink  Ben Beytell  Joseph Birori  Derek Bochard  Lesley Boggs  Alessandro Bonora  Peter Borchert  Sarah Borchert  Markus Borner  Jan Broekhuis  Mark Broodryk  Rob Burns  Peter Bus  Gibson Chanpa  Julius Chinkumba  Marvellous Chisendo  Carol Coppinger  John Coppinger  Hendry de Waal  Garret de Vries  Carmen Dilgee  Clinton Dilgee  Saba Douglas-Hamilton  Christine du Plessis  Nardus du Plessis  Jan du Preez  Pierre du Preez  Mary Duncan  Sarah Durant  Dries Engelbrecht  Henriette Engelbrecht  Christian Eschelten  Chris Eyre  Mike Fay  Ole Friede  Nick Galpine  Jonathan Gibson  Danny Govender  Eve Gracie  Brian Graham  Jan Graham  Moshe Gunikwe  Anne Hadingham  Dave Hamman  Justin Hando  Matthew Harding  Helene Heldring  Marna Herbst  Alweet Hlungwani  Markus Hofmeyr  Andy Hogg  Sean Ingles  Brian Jackson  Murray Jackson  Chris Johns  MK Jones  Simeon Josiah  Beverly Joubert  Dereck Joubert  Jenny Joubert  Joseph Kampamba  Immanuel Kapofi  Ian Khama  Daniel Kashu  John Kayihura  Cathy Kays  David Kays  Dewald Keet  Brandon Kemp  Timothy Khozah  Stella Kimei  Tamlin Kluckow  Grant Knight  Mike Knight  Brigit Kötting  Shayne Kötting  Stephan Kritzinger  Andrew Kruiper  Jennifer Lalley  Daniel Lambert  Mannie le Roux  Bruce Lesley  Debbie Logan  Hilton Loon  Jacqui Loon  Rudi Loutit  Sean Lues  Titus Maasay  Dalton Mabasa  William Mabasa  David Mabunda  Ken Maggs  Johan Malan  Poster Malongwa  Raman Marais  Khosi Maseko  Albert Mashaba  Tammie Matson  Ian McCallum  Sharon McCallum  Tico McNutt  Ian Michler  Rob Moffett  Arddyn Moolman  Catherine Moore  Randall Moore  Estelle Morkel  Pete Morkel  Ntesang Mothanka  Sascha Mueller  Lloyd Mashuri  Mathews Mushumulumbe  Johnny Mwanje  Jazz Nariandas  Petrus Naufiku  Lucy Nhlapo  Isaiah Nyirenda  Johann Oelofse  Louis Olivier  Maika Olkerii  Daniel Parmat  Peter Pearlstein  Danie Pienaar  Robin Pope  Angie Rawlinson  Hennie Rawlinson  Alan Root  Christopher Sakala  Michelle Senekal  Solly Senekal  Rose Shabalu  Anup Shah  Manoj Shah  Patrick Shorten  Michael Sibalatani  Bonny Simataa  Margarida Pires Simoes  Benson Siyawareva  Noreen Siyawareva  Edward Snyders  Sacha Toronyi  Raymond Travers  Isaskar Uahoo  Kevin van Breda  Nico van der Walt  Sorina van der Walt  Elsabe van der Westhuizen  Hugo van der Westhuizen  Dave van Smeerdijk  Landi van Wyk  Freek Venter  Wilfred Versveld  Emsie Verwey  Albertus Vilander  Keith Vincent  Alex Walker  Kobus Wentzel  Deborah White  Ian Whyte  Hayley Wittridge  Owen Wittridge  Grant Woodrow  Brian Worsley  Don Young  Dickson Zimba  Veronica Zulu

Our thanks to you, and the many others whom we encountered more briefly, for your part in the making of this book.

# PREFACE

The fieldwork for this book was, for Beverly and me, a treasure hunt. There is, of quantifiable things, nothing we cherish more – no gold, no oil, no shiny object that we hold more precious, that we seek, that we would touch or look upon, that we revere in our thought, that we treasure more than wilderness.

There is no greed in it, no selfish desire to hoard. You cannot hold what is wild but you can touch it, although as often the opposite seems true. To some extent I think it stems from being alone, from having the opportunity to meet yourself again in a primal sense. Where else can we be more honest, where else is the truth more plain than within ourselves? To stand alone in a primordial place is to have all our vestiges stripped from us. You can carry all the stuff we swathe ourselves in for our esteem to the wilderness – our material possessions, the persona we cultivate and show to others, the special laugh, our involvement in and concern for important things, who has slept in our bed or whose dinner we have shared – but there is nothing in wilderness to acknowledge the stuff of humans. Standing alone in it, our stuff falls away. We become naked again.

To the Maasai, who largely choose to live in an intimate association with wilderness, we are not the people with the shiny aeroplane, or the beautiful teeth or the luxurious coat, but we are the people too uptight to break wind. Alone in the wilderness we become stripped to our essential selves, and I believe that it is only when we confront our very core that we become capable of loving who we are. We are blemished, flawed, full of faults, but it is exactly this that gives us our individuality and it is our individuality that makes each of us unique and thereby beautiful.

We are clever too. Our cleverness has distanced us from the land, both by design and by default. We have cocooned ourselves from the elements in houses and made the earth small with our cars and our jets and the Internet. We have reduced our endeavour for food through a community in which we trade our skills with those of others, and the cost has been huge.

But life is not easy and the earth is not small. Fulfilment comes in small doses whilst hardship seems to endure. I have laughed more than I have wept, but I remember the tears just as well. There is, too, a great deal I have learned standing outside in a storm that was not about the weather. And so I have on occasion stood in wilderness and, on looking outward, have also been looking in and have wondered if we have learned anything at all.

Our cleverness has led us insidiously on a separatist path. It has happened so gradually that still we do not see it, but it is so ingrained that even under duress we cannot think otherwise. We are not of the world, we are the world. We are not animals, we are cleverer than all animals, we are the masters. The earth is ours. Everything on the earth is subject to our command. We know, we chose and we have carved our idols in our own image. Our gods are concerned for us.

But we are wrong. Just as those clever men of the nineties, who decided that a wilderness that was economically viable was a justifiable wilderness, were wrong. There are bigger things than us, things outside of an assignable worth. Things beyond greed, beyond more, beyond might and beyond self. Things that simply are; things of wonder, things of mystery, things sublime and, if you let them in, you will find in them both a gentle and a powerful side.

It is bewitching, for they are bigger than we are and yet they do not command. And, in cupping their waters to our face, we can see our life small and frangible dancing there and, holding it still, the surface will calm and there will come the reflection of the eyes and shining through them the furious power of being alive. And perhaps this is justification enough for wilderness. The fact that we can occasionally walk to the edge of humility and look in and see our place. Or, too, that in the wilderness the question of meaning, of purpose, seems less important and we are more content with being and perhaps in that resignation we approach more closely, caress, however briefly, a sense of the divine.

But perhaps this is all vanity and posturing, for wilderness does not exist for us. Wilderness was here before we came. Wilderness is the sanctuary for all that is instinctive, fundamental, all that is in its living, beyond considered purpose and design. Wilderness is the safety deposit box of time.

Wilderness has an intrinsic value in that it is the repository for a wisdom greater than our own; a wisdom that understands the order of chaos, a wisdom deduced from more time than we can comprehend, that graced the earth for eons before we even began to perceive it, the wisdom of evolution, the wisdom of chance in the arena of time.

We are too rushed for that, we expect change in the span of our lifetime and we are accustomed to profiling all things towards our needs. As a result, virtually the only wild land left is too hostile to inhabit, or land which in its wild state we can utilise. The utilisation of wild land by human beings eventually boils down to money, and it is surprising in retrospect that the architects of the utilisation argument did not see fit to bring their proposal full circle, for there is never enough money, there is always an opportunity for a little more. Wilderness then becomes not a sanctuary at all, but a place trammelled by human beings.

Strangely though, as we sat coated in dust in the Ngorongoro Crater as the 30th vehicle sped past us between the lion and the rhino, I came to realise that the wilderness was still right there, that it was just the presence of we men, with our roads and our vehicles and our behaviour towards the land that had altered what was wild. Remove us and the scene reverted. Wilderness, I thought then, must be a place that man does not go to. I have subsequently softened, perhaps because I have realised that it would be too magnanimous a deed to expect man to respect a wild piece of land purely because it was wild.

I was, however, jubilant when I learnt that the South African National Parks Board has promulgated a law that, where possible, land within its jurisdiction is to be proclaimed wilderness. It is to be land free from all human interference – no roads, no structures, no vehicles. A place to be visited, if at all, on foot, to walk in and then to walk away, leaving nothing at all but wilderness.

It is a far-sighted law that has come only in the nick of time. Wilderness is one of the earth's most precious commodities; there is so little of it left. Each day there is less, but we do not worry about it as we do oil or uranium, for it does not, for now, bear on our every day with such urgency, but it will. The Kruger National Park is not yet 100 years old. In the first year of its proclamation, 16 visitors entered the gates. In 2007, more than one million people crossed its threshold. Our perspectives and our priorities change but the earth is finite, it cannot be made more.

We have finished our treasure hunt now. We found more gold than you will ever know, for tomorrow some of it will be gone. There is nothing in the world more precious than wild land.

*Peter Pickford*
*Okavango, Botswana, 2008*

# FOREWORD

I cannot imagine a wilder place in Africa. We're camped at 2 890 metres on the crater floor of an erupting volcano, Ol Doinyo Lengai, sacred mountain of the Maasai people. The floor bubbles with red-hot lava, but I'm at ease because I'm with Maurice Krafft, a pioneer in the business of filming volcanoes. Maurice suggests a walk across a section of cooler, white lava. That sounds like a good idea until I notice his shoelaces have melted. 'It's not a worry,' he says with his French inflection. 'Walk lightly.' He offers to go first, and I follow. It's a test of faith – but no one has better credentials to navigate the floor of an erupting volcano than Maurice. He has filmed more than 150 of them. Soon my bootlaces are melting too, but, like Maurice, I don't care. We camp on a dirt ridge for three days. The nights are breathtaking. The lava glows crimson. The stars sparkle in the clear African sky. I know now why the Maasai named this Tanzanian volcano the Mountain of God. 'Volcanoes are bigger than us,' Maurice said. 'We are nothing compared to them.'

That was in 1988. Tragically, in 1991 Maurice and his wife, Katia, died while filming at Japan's Unzen volcano. A pyroclastic flow unexpectedly swept onto the ridge where they stood. 'I am never afraid,' Maurice once said, 'because I have seen so many eruptions that even if I die tomorrow, I don't care.'

Years later, camped on the Serengeti Plain, I feel close to the sacred mountain, for its nourishing volcanic ash helped create the soil beneath me. And, when I gaze at that spectacular night sky, I think of Maurice – a true explorer who embraced life with curiosity, enthusiasm and passion.

Maurice's spirit will always be with me, but my life has changed. Volcanoes and the wilds of Africa are no longer my workplace. Instead I work in an office, editing *National Geographic* magazine. The most enjoyable part of my job is looking at photographs, made by men and women who share many of Maurice Krafft's qualities. Our photographers are courageous, curious, passionate, and persistent. You'll find those qualities in Peter and Beverly Pickford, who photographed this spectacular book, *African Safari*. With their artistic and eloquent vision, the Pickfords take us on a special journey, a journey made with love.

One of *African Safari*'s closing photographs is an aerial view of the Ol Doinyo Lengai crater. I can't see the spot where Maurice and I camped, but that was nearly 20 years ago, and the crater floor is higher now. And that pleases me. Our modern world of global travel and instant communication may be shrinking, but the Maasai's sacred mountain is still growing.

*Chris Johns*
*Editor,* National Geographic

---

**PAGES 2 & 3** *A breeding herd of elephant drink from a remote artesian spring in the flat country of Etosha, Namibia.*
**PAGES 6 & 7** *Chitabe Trails Camp. Okavango, Botswana.*

UGANDA

KENYA

RWANDA

TANZANIA

ZAMBIA

ZIMBABWE

BOTSWANA

NAMIBIA

SOUTH
AFRICA

# AFRICA

1. Kruger and the Private Reserves
2. Kgalagadi and the Central Kalahari
3. Etosha, Damaraland and Kaokoland
4. Okavango Delta and Moremi
5. Chobe, Linyanti and Savuti
6. Mana Pools and the Zambezi
7. North and South Luangwa
8. Ngorongoro and the Serengeti
9. Masai Mara
10. Amboseli, Tsavo – East and West
11. The Virungas

# CONTENTS

# SOUTH AFRICA

## Kruger & The Kgalagadi

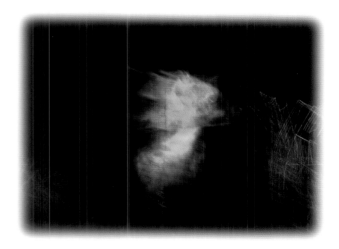

**PAGE 10** *Elephants wade their namesake river. Olifants River, central Kruger National Park.*

**PAGES 12/13** *Crocodiles congregate* en masse *on an isolated sandbank in one of the most remote sections of the park. Olifants River Gorge, central eastern Kruger National Park.*

**ABOVE & LEFT** *In a blur of nervous apprehension, a young spotted hyaena waits beneath a leopard resting between feeds, on a full-moon night in the Sabi Sabi Game Reserve.*

**FOLLOWING SPREAD** *Lanner Gorge, in the baobabed land of the northern park, is cut by the Luvuvhu River through hills of domed rock to create one of the park's most singular landscapes.*

# KRUGER & THE PRIVATE RESERVES

There is a single broad white line painted beside the road as the road pitches downward to begin its descent to the river. The line is not a road marker, it is an indicator, a flood-water indicator. We have encountered several beside the rivers of the Kruger and each time I see them I am reminded of confidence, a wild, shatterproof confidence. Confidence, that impenetrable, close-fitting, luxurious garment of youth that cannot be torn away, cannot be deflated by the thousand small punctures of life, that buoys us up through the wild sea, so that each time we are drawn to the excitement of the storm and pass through the tempest unscathed, we turn and look back through eyes bright with excitement and say to ourselves, 'See!' We look upon our invincible selves until we believe unswervingly, with an almost religious conviction, ingrained as fact, that disaster belongs to another world, not to us.

I was filled with that confidence as I climbed aboard a tiny three-metre inflatable boat and pulled hard on the starter rope, firing the outboard into life. It was the early 1980s and we were working on a private reserve that bordered the Kruger National Park. The boundary between the reserve and the Kruger was the Sabie River and it was in flood. The river had already risen more than three metres above its normal course and, beneath a heavy sky which made a twilight of the day, it was still raining. In the pauses between the squalls, the leaves dripped constantly onto ground that could absorb no more. Water was everywhere and everything was wet. The roads were impassable and we had abandoned our Land Rovers on high ground, between fords now too deep to cross, and traipsed back in the warm rain, running and diving onto our bellies in the deeper puddles until our clothes, our hair, our skin was stained the pale coffee-colour of the mud. We were cut off, isolated, but it raised no panic, no caution – we were swept along by the heady madness of the elements which were, for a time, gone berserk.

The river was 80 to 100 metres wide now and, as ranger Mike Pearson pushed the boat away from the bank and jumped in ahead of me, I

gunned the craft onto a plane. We gave no thought to the crocodiles or the pods of hippopotamus or the giant trees whose branches speared the surface and railed briefly at the sky with their bare, bony joints before being pulled down and on by the great sweep of the water. We saw only the broad tossing back of the beast, which had appeared so suddenly on our doorstep, and went out to ride it with the taste of adrenalin metallic in our mouths.

It was February then and the paint-line beside the road, before it descends to the river, marks the height of the flood of floods that came nearly two decades later in February 2001. We pause beside it and look across to the far bank. It seems impossible. I cannot conjure up so much water in my imagination. The river is far below and the opposite bank so distant that I need binoculars to watch a troop of vervet monkeys feeding in the trees there.

February. February the unpleasant. Hot, sticky, wet February. The heart and the height of the seven-month-long rainy season. The wet-season February; the season of dripping leaves and puddles and mud and heat and sticky air so thick with humidity it feels as if you could cut it with a knife and force the chunks into your mouth. February, the time of luxuriant, explosive growth. A jealous growth that crowds the vistas and the crannies and draws a verdant green curtain across the world, so that even on the plains a hundred buffalo are little more than glimpses of a shoulder, or a rump, or a horn that cause the taller yellow-stalked grass-heads to sway against the sombre sky. February, when the lions emerge onto the road at dusk because it is the only unimpeded place to walk and lie at midnight, panting in the heat, and insects drone and die in their hundreds beneath lights.

I am glad it is not February now. It is the first days of June and, as we roll down past the indicator line of the flood's height, the air is still chill and crisp with the dawn. The river meanders clean and clear between the faded black, smooth outcroppings of the rocks, spreading into fingers through the passages of yellow sand. The last vestiges of a mist shelter in a bed of reeds downstream as we stop on the low-level bridge to look around. It is too early in the day, too chill, for the crocodiles and hippopotamus to emerge from the water to lie on the sand banks and warm themselves in the sun. It is also not yet hot enough for thirst to drive the breeding herds of elephants, whose tracks I see in profusion on the coarse sand, from the now waterless savannas, where the grass has turned yellow and the marula and the white syringa are etched leafless against the sky.

I love the rivers of the Kruger. I am drawn to them, the African river heart of them; their wide sand beds with the tracks of a lone elephant crossing, their eroded banks sheltered by great trees with the baboons and bushbuck underneath, the sound of their water at night with a hippopotamus pushing through, the whispered conversations of their green reed-beds with tasselled heads stirred by the breeze, their silence, and the crocodiles lying still, whose beady, evil watching can make you shiver in the heat.

The Limpopo in the north, which is not as Rudyard Kipling wrote about it, but trailings of water in a broad sand swathe, like a tide receded from a beach. The Luvuvhu in a country of arid hills and stands of baobabs, cutting through solid rock to create the sheer, secret Lanner Gorge. The Shingwedzi, the heartland of the giant elephant bulls, and the Letaba and the Olifants, the succour and the playground of the breeding herds with their squealing and their shouting and their fearful,

compelling commotion. The Timbavati with its red rock walls, dry in the winter, just pools, passing through a country that makes it the most beautiful of them all. Where I would have a home if I could choose. The Sabie with all its moods, scoured clean by the flood and visited by a parade of man and beast. The Crocodile, 380 kilometres south of the Limpopo, splashing and rushing through the rocks, struggling with the effluent of man and his thirst.

Tomorrow we will fly over some of the rivers at the invitation of the game-capture team. The thought distracts me from today. I am filled with anticipation and imaginings for tomorrow, impatient for its dawn. A hundred years have not yet passed since this national park was proclaimed in 1926 and yet it has in that short time risen to prominence as the leader in wilderness conservation, management and policy in Africa. It has climbed there through planned practical management, through research, through the courage to acknowledge when it was wrong and to change. It has climbed there through considered and inspired thought on the backs of dedicated men and women and, tomorrow, I will meet and engage with some of them. And there is in my anticipation, too, that, as a South African, this vast wilderness, almost the size of Belgium, belongs in part to me. Who has not yearned, just once, for the chance to fly above the earth and look down on the familiar contours of land that is home?

---

**OPPPOSITE, LEFT**  *A single-tusked elephant defies the game-capture helicopter.*

**OPPOSITE, RIGHT**  *A leopard with its baboon prey. Singita Private Game Reserve.*

**THIS PAGE**  *A game-capture veterinarian avoids the swinging horn of a darted rhinoceros; a lion intently watches an open safari vehicle; in the private reserves, leopard sightings are improved by being able to drive off the road.*

**ABOVE**  *A vervet monkey steals fruit. Sabi Sabi Little Bush Lodge, Sabi Sand Game Reserve.*

**OPPOSITE, ABOVE**  *Singita Boulders Lodge, bath and outside shower. Sabi Sand Game Reserve.*

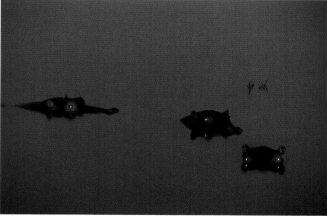

**ABOVE & OPPOSITE** *Dusk in the wilds of Africa is a time for breathing in – a pause – and exhaling slowly. A loitering transition in the foyer of apprehension and expectation between one world and the next.*

**FOLLOWING SPREAD** *Buffalo drink at a seasonal summer stream in the Sabi Sabi Private Game Reserve.*

# TO SAY GOODBYE

The muffled world of my headphones is interrupted by a blast of wind. It is a grating, harsh intrusion, like coarse gravel being drawn across the sensitive microphone. It lasts a second and then is cut off as abruptly as it started. I am left again in the cocooned world of the headphones that is only vaguely breached by the deep drone of the helicopter rotors. I am not surprised by the sound of the wind, I do not even turn around. We are flying with the door open and I have grown accustomed to the sporadic bursts of the wind that drag across Markus's microphone and eddy cold against my back. I keep my eyes fixed on the ground 300 feet below, scanning the terrain through the glass dome that extends from above my head to under my feet. We are searching for white rhinoceros.

A modified shotgun lies across Markus Hofmeyr's knees, its muzzle pointing expectantly out of the open door. Beside him a plastic compartmentalised tray bristles with syringes, vials, sutures, needles and the pink fluffy tails of darts. The wind shrieks again briefly in the headset and the gust plucks a fluffy dart tail from the tray. It flits across my vision, spins crazily in an eddy in the dome ahead of me and then falls to my feet like a dancer exhausted by the frenzy of a final act. I pick it up from the floor and wedge it back in the tray. None of us takes our eyes from the land.

Twice today the shotgun has barked, the modified .22 cartridge propelling a dart heavy and robust enough to pierce the thick hide of a rhinoceros without bending. Twice the dart has flown true and as the helicopter banks and turns I can make out the bulk of the trucks on the road below. Inside, the two young females that succumbed to the sting of the dart wait in a tranquillised state in the darkness of their crates for us to find the final rhinoceros for the day.

It is a crisp June morning in South Africa. Winter. We had flown out in the early light of dawn over a blue land turning yellow, where tendrils of mist traced the twisting of the low land amidst ridges that were set afire by the sun's first kiss. With the sun at our backs, we had flown south-south-west over ridges thick with trees, separated by sand rivers into a land of granite koppies, where lichens glowed lime green and orange on the bald, sand-coloured domes of tumbled stone. Although the dawn was fresh and new, the land below seemed oddly old and the road on which the trucks stood cut through it and reached back beyond today, into South Africa's history.

The road had in its time been the ox-wagon route between the coast and the failed gold-fields of Sabie and Pilgrim's Rest. It was perhaps my thoughts of its history that made the land, seen from above, seem impassive. Not benign, but wise in an inscrutable sort of way that knows that all possession and tenure, all our imaginings, are transient and that through it all change will come. I imagined the promises it had whispered to the eager adventurers of those early years, flush with the fabulous fantasy of gold and the confidence of youth. I sensed its quiet watching as they returned broken and dejected. But not all those men were dejected, not all of those men left: some of those first explorers became more bewitched by the land than the gold, and stayed. One of South Africa's favourite tales, *Jock of the Bushveld*, revolves around one who stayed and travelled that very same road with his dog. I cannot help but find echoes of myself when Percy FitzPatrick, the author of that famous tale, writes, 'The spot always had great attractions for me apart from the big game to be found there. I used to steal along the banks of this lone water and watch the smaller life of the bush. It was a delightful field for naturalist and artist, but unfortunately we thought little of such things, and knew even less; and now nothing is left from all the glorious opportunities but the memory of an endless fascination and a few facts that touch the human chord and will not submit to be forgotten.'

And so, as we flew a grid back and forth across the road, I looked down on the still face of the land and saw not only the land, but its yesterdays too. I had a sense of where it had gone whilst standing still, and it touched a chord in me for the wonder and importance of now. For it is only in the now that we are capable of doing, and it is what we do and what we leave undone that are the foundations of tomorrow.

'Ten o' clock, on top of the ridge,' Markus's voice clear in the headset cuts through my thoughts.

The helicopter banks and drops lower towards the ridge.

'Cow and a calf,' Hendry de Waal, the pilot, says almost absently. We are banking away and I have not even seen them yet. The road passes beneath us again and then I see another group. I only pick them out when we are virtually on top of them, four rhinoceros together, and Hendry swings the helicopter in a wide arc before dropping towards them.

'What do we need?'

'Bull 20 to 25 preferably...'

The wind interrupts '...three 24.'

'The middle one.'

'Got bushes.'

'Coming out.'

The rhino have started to run at our approach.

**OPPOSITE & FOLLOWING SPREAD** *The Wildlife Veterinary Services branch of the South African National Parks is among the most knowledgeable and accomplished wildlife veterinary, capture and translocation teams in the world. It is a measure of its expertise and experience that the air crew will often wager a six-pack with staff on the ground on their ability to have a large mammal finally succumb to sedation on or off a road, making the ground crew's recovery easier and faster.*

'Don't think so.'

'No, not there.'

'That's about 21, 22.'

'22 maybe and the others?'

'You are obviously not talking tons?' I interject. 'Are you looking for an old one?'

'The middle one, Hennie.'

'Ja, got you.'

'His horn size,' says Markus. 'A bull with a horn between 20 and 25 inches.'

The group of rhinoceros is running now and has spread out as it weaves through the thick bush. The rhinoceros that Markus and Hendry are watching is second from the back. The helicopter hangs back, easing the rhinoceros forward but keeping their pace at a trot. I focus on our target through a big lens. It is surprising how light he seems. He trots without effort, a springy bouncing step that belies his bulk. His back is grey-white and I can see a little dust falling from his shoulders in his running. His ears are focused backwards on the racket of the helicopter. He weaves between the trees, his bulk leaning inward on the tight turns like an athlete side-stepping opponents.

'Clearing coming.'

I feel the helicopter angle forward.

'Not yet. This damn thing!'

The helicopter eases back and I watch the rhinoceros slow and hesitate in the clearing. The helicopter is almost stationary, climbing higher.

'Got it. OK.'

The shotgun snaps closed and we swoop down. The rhino picks up his pace and disappears under some thick trees.

'Clearing coming up. Nine o' clock.'

'I'll take him in. Ready?'

'Yep.'

Markus stretches to the end of the special safety harness, leaning out of the open door and bringing the shotgun to his shoulder, to squint down the barrel. The wind scratches at the mike. The bush below is too thick for photographs and I lower the camera. I love this part. The symmetry between the pilot and the vet. It happens fast, too fast for conscious decisions. It is instinctive, the body reacting directly to the mind. No thought, just action, a pure thing. It is the chase, that age-old instinct in every predator's gut, a complete, unwavering focus. And within that focus there is co-operation, consideration of the other's needs, of what is best. It flows without words, just a feeling, a dance that has no steps, no pre-rehearsed score, rather an intimate association brought together by the moment. It is a heady brew, laced with adrenalin.

The helicopter bears around the rhinoceros to turn it towards the clearing. It has been joined by one of the others of the group and they are running shoulder to shoulder. The helicopter remains about 40 metres behind them, keeping their pace at a trot. We are low, a few metres above the trees, the down-draught of the rotors showering a storm of leaves onto the ground. I see a duiker explode from a thicket before the advancing curtain of leaves. Branches flit past just below my feet and we twist slightly to avoid a taller tree. The clearing is approaching and Hendry adjusts his position slightly to get the rhinoceros to try and run along the longest opening. It is still not much of a gap. The rhinoceros are nearing the edge of the trees and the helicopter starts to crowd them. They break into a flat-out charge. The edge of the trees is sharp ahead. We are amongst the trees, weaving. The rhinoceros thunder beneath us. The edge. And we swoop even lower. We are no more than four metres above the coursing grey bodies. The helicopter is flying sideways, completely broadside, offering Markus the best shot. For a second, the aircraft surges upwards and then down again over a lone dead tree. Then, for just a fraction of a moment, it is steady, clear and all there is in the world is the huge, grey back of the beast beneath us. The helicopter shears upwards over the trees as the clearing ends.

'Dart in.'

Hendry presses the transmit button on his joystick.

'Dart in, Marius,' and I know that at the trucks on the ground the stopwatches will be pressed and the big digital figures will start to climb: zero one, zero two, zero three... and it is only then, like a cold brick in my stomach, that I realise why we are catching this rhinoceros bull. My head feels giddy from the shock. It cannot be, but there can be no other reason. I look wildly across at Markus and Hendry, but they are watching the rhinoceros below us. The helicopter is climbing. I look away out over the land punctuated by koppies and outcrops, but I do not see it.

The rhinoceros below us is approaching the road, running about 40 metres parallel to it. Hendry pushes him closer still and then backs away. The rhinoceros slows to a jog. As the digital figures pass the two zero zero mark, the rhinoceros wobbles in his run and slows to a walk.

'Showing signs.'

'Signs, Marius, you can come in,' and the helicopter climbs high into the sky, hovering above the rhinoceros now only 15 metres from the road.

young veterinarian assistant's hands feeling the softness of his lips, running across his skin and resting softly on his side, counting his breaths and the beating of his heart.

I do not know why it is harder to accept the death of a big creature than a small one. The death of an elephant or a buffalo rather than a mouse, or the limp form of a sparrow as opposed to that of an eagle. It should not be different but it is, and I feel it in me now. A weight that makes the coffee drinking entirely mechanical. I think of the Eskimo and the Bushman giving thanks for their kills and, feeling silly but in dead earnest, I whisper a homage to the sky.

I know why we are here. It is a simple rationale and I know, even in my pain, that it is sound. I think back to the late 1800s when Percy FitzPatrick walked this road with his stocky dog. I glance over at the road. Back then every man hunted for the pot, dipping at will for his protein needs and, I am sure,

In the distance I see the dust from the trucks as they start forward. I am hunched in my seat, the camera forgotten on my lap, and I remain there as we land. Markus jumps from the helicopter and sprints forward beneath the blades to attend to his tranquillised charge.

I am riddled with guilt. It was I who spotted him. I am responsible and there is no way out. My gut is screaming. No! I fold my arms to hold it down. Hendry has shut off the motor and slowly the rotors wind to a standstill. He opens my door from the outside.

'Coffee?'

'Thanks.'

I take the small cup and sit on the helicopter skid in the sun as Hendry leaves to go to where the rhinoceros lies. I cannot follow. Cannot watch the

occasionally just for the lust of the kill into the seemingly endless wealth of the wild. But the ranks of men have never grown less, we are always more and through that we persecute the world. In the 1920s when the Sabie and Shingwedzi Reserves were amalgamated to form the Kruger National Park, there were estimated to be less than 60 elephants in the entire park and white rhinoceros were all but locally extinct.

From the earliest days of the Kruger Park's existence, when Colonel Stevenson-Hamilton shot certain predators on sight so that the populations of prey species could flourish, the park embraced a policy of management by interference. People were moved, fences were erected, country was burned, water points were put in and animals were shot. With time, these management principles became less and less the fancy or the whim of the warden and increasingly based on research in the field. Today there are more than 160 active research projects in the park and their impact on the reserve and its management is profound.

Management decisions are backed now by a thorough knowledge of the field. The management-by-interference principle allows theories to be tested. Some have proved to be wrong, but this still leads to the path that is best and the Kruger National Park, in constantly developing its understanding of the wilderness and its management through practice, sets many of the precedents for the

conservation of the wild in Africa. It is consistently at the forefront of the conservation arena and the rhinoceros we have caught today are a fine example.

Before the 1960s, rhinoceros were an uncommon sight in the park and black rhinoceros were far more common than white. Then, during the 1960s, 300 white rhinoceros were introduced into the park in an attempt to re-establish the population that had been decimated by hunters prior to its declaration. The effort was a resounding success and today there are more than 5 000 white rhinoceros in the Kruger. Each year, during winter, when there is less chance of heat stress, a number of rhinoceros

are now captured and sold outside the park. They are expensive, and they donate as their legacy a substantial fund that will help save and protect, will increase our understanding and will make a better future for the park, its denizens and its visitors.

I look through the obscuring trees at the rhinoceros, whose fate I sealed the moment he stood clear of the trees beneath me. Perhaps his legacy will provide radio-tracking collars for the dwindling populations of sable antelope that may help to solve the riddle of their decline; perhaps it will be that his going provides the means to a new understanding of fire and will have ramifications for all the animals of Africa; perhaps he will merely fund anti-poaching patrols and, in giving his life, will save the lives of many others. I feel the guilt welling in me again. I have robbed him of his freedom, taken his life, I have his blood on my hands, for I know it is only the hunter who measures his prize – 20 to 25 inches. I am sad right through. I stand and drain the last of the sweet coffee from the mug and then, squinting through the trees towards the rhinoceros, whisper my thanks once more. A francolin cocks its head at me, curious, cautious, and I grin lopsidedly at it, feeling a little mad. It explodes with a raucous cackle into flight, its wings shining yellow as they catch the sun.

**TOP**  *White rhinoceros on a granite koppie;* **ABOVE**  *Lichtenstein's hartebeest in capture container.*

**OPPOSITE, ABOVE**  *A Lichtenstein's hartebeest from the capture helicopter.*

**OPPOSITE, BELOW**  *The Luvuvhu River emerges from Lanner Gorge. Northern Kruger National Park.*

**FOLLOWING SPREAD, CLOCKWISE FROM LEFT**  *The luxury offered by the private lodges indulges romantic imaginings. Singita Boulders bathroom; Singita Lebombo deck; Boma fantasy at Sabi Sabi; Singita Lebombo.*

**THIS PAGE**  *During winter, the normally dull colours of the Nile monitor intensify and males fight for the right to mate.*

**OPPOSITE**  *A hippopotamus crosses a sandbank towards the sanctuary of the Olifants River in central Kruger National Park.*

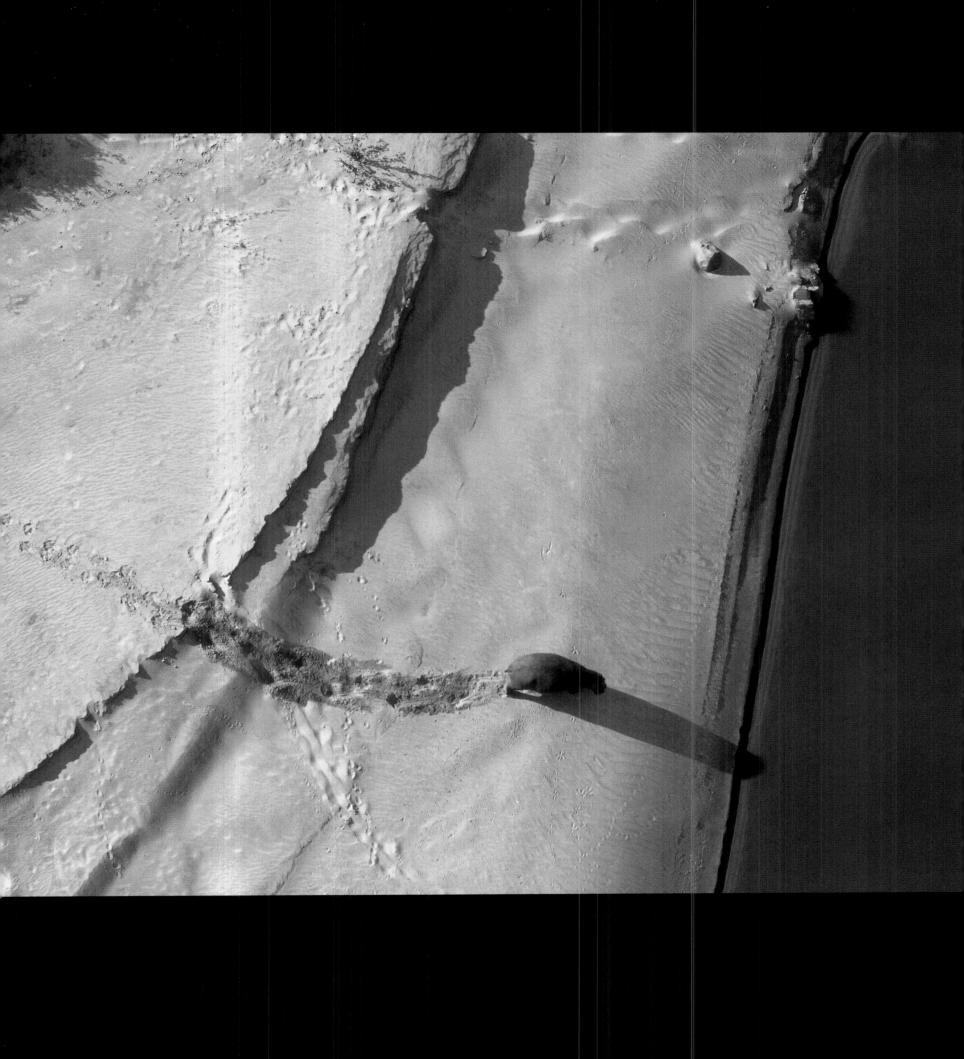

**TOP** *Since their re-introduction to the park in the 1960s, white rhinoceros have made a strong comeback and now number in the thousands.*

**ABOVE & OPPOSITE, ABOVE** *On winter mornings, the Limpopo River, a wide meandering swathe of sand and shallow water, raises a column of mist along the park's northern boundary.*

**OPPOSITE** *Two leopards spar. Singita Private Game Reserve.*

*Years ago, I had an argument with an opinionated visitor to South Africa who had spent much time flying over the country. He felt that South Africa was doomed. He had seen the masses, he had observed the poverty from the air. I argued that you cannot see will and hope, determination and belief. I thought of him as I sat beside this fever tree, felled by fire, in northern Kruger National Park and watched a reedbuck in the distance, scraping away the black ash of burnt grass to reach the fresh green shoots emerging from beneath.*

# KGALAGADI

I was never a good student of the sciences. They were too dry, too bland in their expression, too stolid in their progress to conclusion for my imagination. I prefer things that are like an Italian meal, like Cairo traffic, like a Zulu impi. I was surprised, therefore, when wading through a scientific assessment of the Kgalagadi, to stumble across the word ephemeral. It arrested me. It is almost too soft, too evocative a word for science, it is pretty. 'Ephemeral rivers', it said.

In the strict arena of science, in the use of language without latitude, it was correct. The rivers of the Kgalagadi almost never flow. Even the word flow must be corrected if we are to be precise; flood is more to the mark. The Auob has flooded three times in the past 50 years, the Nossob once. But these are not rivers of water, they are rivers of sand and, in that, they are anything but ephemeral.

Everything about them is suffused with endurance. They are stoic, poised, long suffering, possessed of an immutable awareness of time that reaches far beyond today into geographical history, into permanence. It is as if they are held still, in abeyance, paused in their motion like the dune sea through which they thread their way. It seems almost that, like the stationary troughs and crests of the dunes, they are in anticipation of a time, an event that will once more set them free, cast them once more into motion. But for now they are there as they are, waiting.

In the 40 degree plus Celsius temperatures of summer, when the red sand of the desert is reflected onto the base of the clouds so that all day the sky is tinged with the hue of sunset, the rivers shimmer and dance in the heat. False promises of water are conjured in their distances, warping and contorting the black, stark profiles of the trees, now tall and thin, now squat, until in the receding distance their trunks are severed from the earth to float upwards and then disappear.

It is the trees that hold the age of the land, that are the countenance of its austerity, that are the meters for the desert's slow time. Like all life here, they gather at the places of water, the riverbeds and the springs. Shepherd's trees that stand scattered and alone are reclusive veterans, reluctant of company, their single white-barked trunks standing straight beneath their rounded, dense-leafed tops. Albizia and silver terminalia too, but it is the camel thorns that are the trees of this land. The trees of the dry riverbeds, of the limestone cliffs, of thirst, the trees of the yellow cobra and the red sand, the Kgalagadi trees. The trees that come to mind.

Their bark is deeply fissured, coarse, grey, sometimes almost black. An old skin and weathered like that of an ancient Bushman crone I had met somewhere to the east. Plump, grey-skinned geckos with white spots hide in the deeper crevices and, where branches have been torn from the trunk, the occasional small owl with false, feathered eyes finds a place to hide from the day.

Their leaves are fine, a filigree of green that issues from branches, twisted, convoluted, contorted like hands reaching out from arthritic pain. The trunks somehow emerge sturdy from these first reachings, until their crests often stand more than 10 metres high, seldom straight, leaning outward towards some long-forgotten whim.

And in winter, when the trees are brittle and still beneath stars that appear as frost on the sky and the thermometer approaches ten below zero, you can, in the quiet, hear the sands of the rivers sigh and creak as they settle. It is as if

**OPPOSITE** *Nostrils flaring, a springbok defends its territory.*

they are alive in their waiting, slumbering and anticipating – together with the dormant seeds beneath the surface – their brief release that is the soft kiss of rain.

There is no season of rain in a dry land, no time of certainty, no late or early. The Bushmen do not watch the sky and wait. And yet all the land is waiting. Between November and April, the thunderheads billow and climb into the sky, a performance of white and purple and black that taunts the dry earth and strangles out the rays of the sun. Beneath their heavy bellies, pregnant with promise, lightning cracks its bright whip and, looking up, you wonder if it has begun. But this is perhaps the desert's cruellest hour.

With all the pent-up bitterness of a barren womb, it lashes the earth instead with the malevolent tongue of the wind. It shrieks. It screams across the land. It plucks and tugs at the trees, pushes against them, shaking their dry thorns to fall on the ground. Their branches groan, and all the while the wind whistles, its pitch growing higher. It stirs the

dust in a land-bound cloud before it, plucks the red sand from the crests of the dunes in giant plumes. It raises the very mantle of the earth until all that can see become blind. The world shrinks, closes in, and for each it becomes only a dull, shrouded void, the red-orange opaque curtain beyond. Lions shelter in the lee of the trees, but there is no respite from a tempest that rises from the ground.

Sometimes it ends as abruptly as it began, with a sigh. The clouds retreat, sand trickles to the base of a dune to lie still once more. The gemsbok turn their haunches away from the storm, shake the sand from their ears and depart into the lingering half-world of the dust. They will wait, persevere with the same stoic resignation as the trees. Wait without watching, without counting, wait without anticipation for that ephemeral season of the desert: the season of green, of birth, the time of herds and migrations, and of rain.

You can smell the rain in the desert before it reaches you. You will know. You will smell it on the wind, smell it dissolving into the earth, that distinct aroma of its brew. It draws me out into the open, to watch it come, to breathe it in. I can remember my palms upturned, my face too, my eyes closed, the first gentle splashes, a pause and then the stinging cold tirade, luxurious on my skin.

**ABOVE** *The Verreaux's eagle-owl's habit of bowing to each other prior to egg-laying is anthropomorphically both sombre and delightful.*

**LEFT** *A leopard and her nearly full-grown cub cavort on a fallen tree in the Nossob River bed.*

45

**PREVIOUS SPREAD** *Like a spate river that begins as a trickle an hour or so after dawn, Cape turtle-doves fly in to waterholes to drink. At certain times of year, their numbers can quickly swell to a tumultuous flood. And then, as quickly, they are gone, and by mid-morning the waterholes are still again.*

**THIS SPREAD** *Spotted hyaena, once rare in the Kgalagadi, are on the increase, chasing lions off carcasses and killing as a pack.*

**FOLLOWING SPREAD** *Two lionesses drive off a male that has approached their cubs too closely.*

# IN HIDING

I am walking softly. My footfalls and the gentle creaking of the wooden slats of the walkway sound too loud to my ears, which seek and explore the quiet of the desert night. I reach the deserted hide and sit, grateful for my own silence and, only half looking, concentrate on the clues my ears find in the wide, dry riverbed and the dunes beyond the waterhole.

Against the black luminescence of the sky, I can make out the darkest silhouettes of the taller thorn trees with their spreading crowns. Through the lingering dust of the day's violent sandstorm the stars glow with a yellow, candle-like cast. It seems strange when I realise that I can hear the silence of this night.

My eyes are scratchy and tired from the harsh light of the day that bleached all colour from the land. A light delivered by a sun that, despite its intensity, had failed to drive the chill from the breeze that had grown to a gale. The wind had torn at the land as if with intent, lifting sheets of sand and driving the finer dust of the riverbeds into billowing clouds that shrouded the continuity of the world, revealing only curtained moments where life appeared stoic, suffering and yet strangely determined before the onslaught of the storm.

The storm has abated completely now and, although I can still discern a fine grit against my teeth, the sand and the dust have mostly settled once more to the ground. I listen attentively for signs of the life I had witnessed, so resigned to the misery of the storm. Life that had seemed, now in retrospect, so certain that this still night would come.

I hear footfalls approaching along the walkway to the hide. Beverly joins me and, straddling the bench where I am sitting, draws close till her knee presses against mine. She lays her head against my shoulder and we sit like that, still in the quiet of the night.

For a long time nothing happens and then, in the periphery of my vision, I see something moving. It is approaching the water with caution, trotting forward and then stopping to look and listen. It is a small creature, and it is only when it nears the edge that I am able to make out that it is a bat-eared fox.

A few metres from the water it pauses again, its large ears twisting and probing the night. Suddenly it skips forward in fright and spins around, staring hard into the dark, its unmoving ears cocked forward.

Drinking in the desert, I have learnt, is a dangerous time, fraught with ambush and conflict, and I have noticed that even the brazen spotted hyaena pauses before lowering its head to the water, where it is at its most exposed and vulnerable.

The bat-eared fox stands motionless for more than a minute before deciding that the danger is imagined, then trots to the water and, with a short quick lapping, begins to drink. It drinks for a surprisingly long time, keeping its head to the water and scanning for danger with ears sensitive enough to hear beetle larvae moving underground.

To the sound of its lapping I muse that, on a grander scale, the Kalahari has been much as this night. Initially the country is seemingly empty and yet there is something in it that is filled with anticipation, as if the land itself, in its quietude, is holding something back. It seems timeless, possessed with an enduring patience, and there is nothing hurried or rushed in it. It is only when one has learnt this and stops looking over the land, learnt to pause and rather look at it, that the desert begins to reveal itself, fragment by precious fragment.

In contemplating the landscape of the Kalahari it defies being described as harsh or even austere for it is not a barren desert. The broad snaking of its dry riverbeds and pans are fringed and punctuated by old and statuesque trees and the endless ridges and valleys of its red dune sea are topped with golden grass that make it more beautiful and serene than severe. It is rather the elements that punish, mould and worry it that make it a harsh place. Even on the most benign days they are a constant presence, altering the character of the land.

From an almost constantly cloudless sky, the sun sears the colours from the land until one is left at its zenith with an almost white light, suitable only for bleaching bones, and the desperate drive of thirst. It is only at the edges of its presence, at dawn and dusk, that the sun holds a gentler sway. But these times are brief and, as dusk fades to night, the vault of the stars seems to suck the heat from the earth with a suddenness that is surprising and a thoroughness that reduces many nights to a bitter battle to stay warm.

The wind, too, when it comes, seems set on violence. Blasting the fragile sands from the desert's surface, it raises them to the sky until an opaque shroud blankets the moaning torments of the ground. In the

**TOP** *Kgalagadi Tented Camp in a lightning storm.*

**OPPOSITE** *Peter and Audrey Fowler, whose bright camp flies in the face of the more neutral tones of safari tradition, enjoy the intimacy of a warm shelter on a cool night.*

riverbeds the finer dust creates a solid, hot fog that trickles sand through every crevice and crack until it seems that the very caverns of one's sanity are being invaded.

The elements bring to the Kalahari a torment which gnaws at our discomfort and yet I found that when they had passed I had survived, that I had, in a way, overcome. It seemed to me too that I was not alone in this overcoming, that the land itself seemed in repose after the onslaught. I had become aware, through these shared trials by fire, as it were, of a growing affinity with the land, of an imagined unity of experience drawing me closer to the predators, the antelope, the smaller creatures and the birds of this desert. In this affinity I found, too, in myself, a greater willingness to pause, to let the smallest moment have its time, and I became absorbed

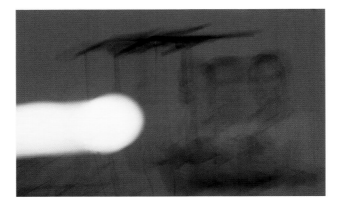

by what at first had seemed a barren landscape.

I had seen two children lying on the hot sand in front of a ground squirrel, whose burrow was shrouded by a shrub laden with white blossoms, and I was delighted to recognise in myself the same unblemished capacity for awe and wonder. Perhaps it is merely this return to something of our essential selves that makes us fond of a place, but there is to my mind a more complex transformation that occurs.

I thought of the few Bushmen families in the Central Kalahari Game Reserve who, at the time of writing, were embroiled in a legal battle to remain on their land within the reserve. Many of the communities of Bushmen in the Central Kalahari had been persuaded (some say bribed and manipulated) to leave the land, but a few had chosen to remain.

I had wondered at the root of the conviction of a man who would stand and fight for what seemed so little. In my deepening association with the desert I realised that I had climbed onto the first step of what must be to these men their Tower of Babel. I saw then that they where not from the desert, they were of it. I could in my imagination extend this thought to the point where the union between a man and his earth was complete. And in my thinking I came to understand that there existed in the Kalahari a community in which man separated himself neither from the animals nor the land, in which his part was not aloof and separate but integral and intimate.

The creeping chill of the night brings me back from my reverie. The bat-eared fox has finished drinking and is standing beside the water, staring motionless into the night beyond. A single riffle of a breeze stirs the long, dense fur of his coat and then he moves off at a light trot, quickly swallowed by the dark.

The presence of the night looms all around, a dark void, but I am learning that in nothingness there is always possibility, the anticipation of something, and knowing it makes it hard to move away.

**ABOVE** *Marna Herbst, a researcher, tracks African wild cat movement, and Andrew Kruiper, last of a lineage of traditional desert trackers.*

**OPPOSITE, ABOVE** *A flight of red-billed quelea;* **BELOW** *Springbok in the rain.*

**PAGE 56, ABOVE** *Lion at dusk;* **BELOW** *A cheetah stalks.*

**PAGE 57, ABOVE** *Bibron's gecko on the canvas roof of a tent;* **BELOW** *Two porcupines huddle successfully in a defence against lions.*

**ABOVE** *A group of kudu at a waterhole in the Central Kalahari Game Reserve, Botswana.*

**OPPOSITE** *The Kgalagadi Transfrontier National Park, in South Africa and Botswana, together with its neighbour the Central Kalahari Game Reserve in Botswana, offers lions a range through some of the most remote countryside in southern Africa.*

**FOLLOWING SPREAD** *The Nossob River bed. Kgalagadi Desert.*

# NAMIBIA

## Etosha, Damaraland, Kaokoland

*Chris Eyre is one of the conservationists we most admire. Unswervingly dedicated, inventive, fair and outspoken, but shy of the limelight, he has stood for his conviction in the face of extreme peer pressure and, while his country was still divided by racial laws, he embraced community participation long before it became wise practice elsewhere in the world. At the end of his tenure as conservator of Kaokoland, the Himba people gave him the land that was one of his favourite camp sites. He remains the only outsider ever to receive this honour.*

# ETOSHA
## DAMARALAND & KAOKOLAND

It is quite easy on a system of good gravel roads, amidst the convenience of a well-appointed rest camp, to forget the tenor of the land. In an air-conditioned cocoon with hot and cold water, with electricity, we are apt to overlook it. We do not consider the land, we are only peripherally aware of it, we have smoothed it over, made it approachable, provided for its hardships, made it tame. Today, names like Dorsland, Stinkwater, Nêrens, Bitterwater mean little to us, they are just names, not warnings or signs of hope. We pass them with cursory interest on our way to more exotic temptations: Leeudrink, Olifantsbad, Wolfsnes. But the land has not changed, it is still there. The same land, a thirst-land, a land where there was a nothing so infinite that it became a name, 'Nêrens', a land where even bitter or stinking water was important. An immutable wild land, indifferent, and the animals know it as we no longer do.

Recently a guide set out into this land. A guide of the gravel roads and the rest camps. A guide who could point out a springbok, a lion and an elephant and tell you the facts he had learnt, the anecdotes he had heard. 'There are no monkeys in Etosha.' But he had never stopped to wonder why, never looked for reasons or tried to understand, never really felt in his own gut the thirst that made the elephants run the last few hundred metres to the water. He had seen, but he had learnt by rote – he did not know the land and, dangerously, this he did not comprehend.

He drove a small bus with a group of mostly older clients and, on a special permit, entered the tourism-restricted area of Western Etosha. It was summer and the rain had been plentiful. I was not there, but I can imagine it in my mind's eye: the clients still drowsy from being awoken early, amused at the uninspiring gate of the western entrance, the dilapidated camp beside it, the woman guard with enormous breasts squeezed into a uniform a size too small, the guide irritated by her unhurried propriety, her pedantic scrutiny of their documents, the clearly lingering look she gives the cooler box which holds their lunch as they depart her lonely outpost.

The extreme west of Etosha is a rocky country of sharp hills that quickly gives way to the flat savanna and occasional low rise of the rest of the reserve. The bush, once clear of the hills, is short and scrubby and under summer's green mantle it is dense. I imagine them lucky to find a small group of the rare Hartmann's zebra drinking from a pool at the edge of the road. I see, too, the guide failing to notice the fresh pug marks of a leopard that drank at the same pool. Pug marks that lead a few hundred metres down the road to the clear drag marks of where the leopard pulled its duiker kill towards a distant tree. An opportunity missed. He has good eyes, he spots game, but his experience is the luxury of a voyeur. He is not intuitive, he has not learnt to find things.

Later, he again fails to notice the tracks of a breeding herd of elephant that has crossed the road toward the north and, shortly thereafter, the tracks of an even bigger herd that are fresher still, the passageways where they have marched in a line having flattened the tall grass. He does not stop to listen. He cannot, through his closed window, catch the distinctive odour of their fresh dung. He has not

**PAGE 62**  *A pride of lion loiters at a spring on the edge of Etosha Pan, keeping thirsty Burchell's zebra at bay.*

**PAGES 64/65**  *'Self painted'. The white clay of a rainwater pan coats one of Etosha's large solitary bull elephants after a mud bath.*

**PAGES 66/67**  *Kathetaura Tjiningere. On the day we first met him, he had walked nearly 80 kilometres through the trackless Kaokoveld Desert. Near Etanga, Kaokoland.*

considered that it is summer, a good, wet summer when the plethora of rainwater pans frees the elephants from their dependency on the permanent waterholes of the dry winter season. He has read about the elephants of Etosha that move north and east out of the park during wet summers, but he has not considered their moving, has not placed himself on their journey, has not grasped their passing through the land. And so the land remains barren, its nuance, its content unseen.

He has been daydreaming, lulled into reverie by the smooth course of the road, the repetitive monotony of the wall of tall grass and dense scrubby trees. Summer guiding is harder, he knows that. In the dry winter the animals are reliant on the permanent waterholes, forced into concentration around them, and game viewing is a simple affair of plotting a course between the waterholes of one's choice. He has his favourites – Okaukuejo, right in the camp, where you can sit in the open, he does not even have to drive; Sueda and Salvadora, flush on the edge of the Etosha Pan, a morning's drive from Halali Rest Camp, where he has spotted most of the cheetah he has seen; Klein Namutoni, a short drive from Namutoni Camp where, if he leaves as the gates open, he can catch hyaena drinking there, and then the Tamboti Forest loop, beyond which one finds the tiny dik-dik.

He is hopeful for his time at Namutoni now. A friend has told him of a jackal's den near Twee Palms, which he will keep secret until then. The herds should be there too, on the plains around Fischer's Pan. His clients always love the fort, that crisp white building with its square ramparts and tiny rooms, its bougainvillaea and palms, so spruce, so fairytale that even the yellowed images in its museum cannot make real the terror, the blood in the earth of 1904 when the Owambo attacked and razed its predecessor to the ground.

He is distracted from his reverie by the niggling concern that they have seen no game for a while. He glances over at his youngest client, a woman in loose summer shorts in the seat just behind him. She blushes lightly, smiles and, on a whim, he slows and, ignoring the bold no entry sign, turns from the main road onto a track. It is not a

tourist road, it is a ranger's patrol track, narrow, winding, puddled. Immediately the land draws closer.

Bushes drag along the side of the vehicle, the wheels slip and spin, throwing smears of mud against the windows. He is excited at first, breaking new ground, forging ahead, closer to the heart of something. He can feel it. Twice he turns onto other unmarked tracks, but after more than an hour they have still seen no animals and then, on a bend in the road, the wheels slide out of control. They teeter for a moment on the edge of a gully before sliding in to become stuck. Not all the clients muck in to dig the vehicle free, but those who do, use precious drinking water to wash themselves clean.

He knows he should turn back. He tastes the first seed of doubt, feels the first nervous spasm in his gut that he is lost. But he is the guide, that is the image of himself he carries in his head. He has more than a hundred years of history behind him in Africa. He just cannot turn back.

Three months later, the ranger backs his four-wheel-drive up and attaches a heavy chain to the small bus where it sits forlorn in the now dry, cloying embrace of the clay, its final stop, the third time it got stuck. Everything else is gone. Blown away are the crumbs of the biscuits they shared for dinner, too scared to think to save some for the days ahead. Dissolved into the grass and the clay is the diarrhoea of those who waited behind, caused by having to drink the muddy water of the pools. Removed is the T-shirt left at a junction less than a kilometre from the main road. And washed away are the footprints that turned from it, gone the wrong way, stumbling from exhaustion for another day and a half before the ranger found them, with two hyaena following close behind. The bus creaks and groans as it breaks free. Its protest is soft in the vastness of the land, swallowed by the quiet, unheard, except perhaps by the unseen animals.

**ABOVE**  *A lion peers from his ambush in the lee of a water trough.*

**OPPOSITE**  *Burchell's zebra stallions clash as drying surface water forces herds together at waterholes.*

**FOLLOWING SPREAD**  *Burchell's zebra drink by the light of the moon.*

*No! There's the land (Have you seen it?)*
*It's the cussedest land that I know,*
*From the big, dizzy mountains that screen it;*
*To the deep, deathlike valleys below.*
*Some say God was tired when He made it;*
*Some say it's a fine land to shun;*
*Maybe: but there's some as would trade it*
*For no land on earth – and I'm one.*

Robert Service
THE SPELL OF THE YUKON

**TOP**  *Himba women dance. Orupembe, Kaokoveld Desert.*

**OPPOSITE, ABOVE, & ABOVE**  *The Damaraland Desert seems to resonate like a wind-strummed taut wire whenever one's eye pauses on its vast vistas.*

**OPPOSITE, BELOW**  *Christiaan Bakkes, storyteller extraordinaire, read us poetry beside the fire in the desert night. Damaraland.*

**TOP**  *Waterhole watching at night is a highlight of Etosha National Park. Three black rhinoceros drink before an electric storm.*

**ABOVE**  *Black rhinoceros, the smaller of Africa's two rhinoceros species and more inclined to charge.*

**OPPOSITE**  *Moths in flight.*

**FOLLOWING SPREAD**  *Southern giraffe approach an artesian spring at dusk.*

# BOTSWANA

## Okavango, Chobe & Linyanti

# OKAVANGO & MOREMI

It is the start of summer and sweltering. For yet another day we wait amidst wavering lines of animals standing patiently, heads down. We wait for the thunderstorm promised by the envoy of dark, roiling cumulus clouds that from time to time blot out the sun and cast shadows across the plain. Our eyes are drawn to the sky and we search for the scent of rain in the thick, feverish air. It is December, just short of Christmas, and the rains are late.

In past years we have chosen to travel in Botswana during the mild, clear-sky months of April and September. Earlier this same year we had heard that the floodwaters of the Okavango had reached as far south as Lake Ngami. It was the first time in 30 years that Lake Ngami had filled and the new water had drawn millions of quelea and waterbirds to fresh feeding grounds. So, in wintry June, we had made a long detour through Lake Ngami and the Central Kalahari Desert en route to the Kgalagadi Transfrontier Park.

Our days at Lake Ngami had passed quickly and each chilly dawn found us huddled closely around our campfire until, like a giant paintbrush sweeping across the sky and blackening out the sun, the quelea would suddenly appear. Perhaps I took too many pictures as we traipsed for kilometres through the shallow water, seeking the image that would tell this unusual story. By midday my eyes were red and stinging from the glare off the water and the harshness of the sun, and it was a physical relief when, in the late afternoon the quelea, their thirst satiated for another day, faded to their distant roosts as abruptly as they had arrived.

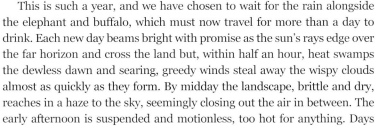

Now, in the breath-stealing desperation of the summer heat, we had returned to Botswana for the season of the storms. In good years of almost year-round water, brought in the winter months by the seasonal flood from Angola and the summer rainfall, the Okavango is for the most part a quiescent, watery paradise. But in years of a meagre winter flood and late arrival of the summer rains, there is drought and hardship.

This is such a year, and we have chosen to wait for the rain alongside the elephant and buffalo, which must now travel for more than a day to drink. Each new day beams bright with promise as the sun's rays edge over the far horizon and cross the land but, within half an hour, heat swamps the dewless dawn and searing, greedy winds steal away the wispy clouds almost as quickly as they form. By midday the landscape, brittle and dry, reaches in a haze to the sky, seemingly closing out the air in between. The early afternoon is suspended and motionless, too hot for anything. Days become weeks.

Then, one random afternoon, the storm comes. Black clouds gather quickly and water falls on the land, not as drops of rain but in broad sheets that shut out our vision and threaten to drown our open Land Rover. We wrap our waterproof camera bags in layers of canvas on the seats. The floor is awash with the muddy torrent and in a blind frenzy, tinged with panic, we painstakingly attempt to work our way to the protection of some tall trees, avoiding the deep ruts of rushing water. Lightning, in sharp bright bolts, is making direct arrows from the sky to our trees. There is no thought of taking pictures and I am wondering how long the food we packed in a small cooler box for the day will last if we are stranded, as no one knows our whereabouts and our vehicle tracks will be obliterated by the deluge. We are reduced to two small sets of eyes peering out from layers of sodden canvas. Water seeps down our necks into our clothes and shoes, and I watch opaque sheets of rain blanket our world that is dissolving in ever-changing patterns.

After a few hours the rain eases to a soft and constant falling and, calmer now, I become ecstatic with the knowledge that a new season has begun. We throw off our canvas cocoons and go out into the rain. We wade the tiny rivers flowing around the high ground and, with wet hands, I help a tortoise to safety. Like the first day of creation, butterflies unrobe the dull fetters of their pupae and spread their rainbowed wings; urgent termites emerge from the earth to find their mates and build anew in the soft earth. Today, food and water are brought to the Okavango, calves will be born and grow fat, elephants will migrate away from the perennial

PAGE 92 *A lion crosses a typical Okavango Delta floodplain. Mombo;* PAGES 94/5 *Summer rains often fall in a deluge and left this tortoise in deep water. Chief's Island;* PAGES 96/97 *A hippopotamus threat is well heeded. Encountered in the frequent, narrow channels of the Delta with little room to manoeuvre or escape, they have a propensity to attack. Chitabe;* PAGES 98/99 *A mokoro poler crosses the seasonal lagoon in front of Xigera Camp;* OPPOSITE, TOP *An elephant bull eats fruit fallen from a tree that shades the camp. Mombo;* MIDDLE *This handcrafted bridge over a permanent channel of clear water is a landmark destination for overland safaris. Third Bridge, Moremi Game Reserve;* BOTTOM *Documentary filmmakers Beverly and Dereck Joubert are known for their passionate involvement in Botswana's conservation policies.*

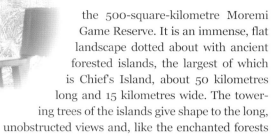

rivers to faraway forests, and zebra and wildebeest will march in search of new grass where the dry pans have been flushed with water. Trees will become bright with flower and fruit and the summer migrant birds will arrive from Europe and elsewhere in Africa to bring a rush of activity and colour to their branches. Like a full-moon tide, the tension of the dry brown season will be washed over with the softer, tranquil hues of green and blue.

In a year of good rain, pans and channels will provide water until the floodwaters from the Angola rains arrive, via the Cubango, Quito and Kavango rivers, to flow into the Okavango River and to replenish the waters of the Delta. The water spreads into a fan of channels and floodplains and travels 250 kilometres to eventually, via the Boro Channel and the Thamalakane River, arrive around June in the frontier safari town of Maun at the southern end of the Delta. And thus, via rain and the floodwaters of the Okavango River's delta, life is brought to an otherwise dry Kalahari Desert.

Nearly one fifth of Botswana is given over to game reserves and Botswana's safari industry is thriving with its 'low volume, less interference' conservation policy. Almost the entire expanse of the Okavango Delta falls into protected wilderness areas, at the core of which lies the 500-square-kilometre Moremi Game Reserve. It is an immense, flat landscape dotted about with ancient forested islands, the largest of which is Chief's Island, about 50 kilometres long and 15 kilometres wide. The towering trees of the islands give shape to the long, unobstructed views and, like the enchanted forests of fairytales, they burst with life.

It was with the anticipation of adventure that we drove the dusty two-track road the length of Chief's Island to eventually arrive at the storm in the Mombo area.

Even though Botswana's inland delta changes every year according to the level of the flood, the Okavango remains a constant wildlife haven. It is blessed with warm weather and a harmonious people who are prone more to discussion than confrontation. And the camps here are a testimony to their sensibilities – they are built of natural materials with a stringently applied non-permanent imprint, and the wood and canvas structures incline nature in. You sleep to the sound of hippopotamus and lion in a darkness that is spun with stars and you waken to the bustle of the birds' dawn feeding. Light comes in soft layers of orange and blue through the mesh windows of your tent, enticing you out to see what surrounds you and, I have found, some of what you see, something of what you find, is mirrored back within yourself.

**OPPOSITE & TOP**  *During the Delta's flood in the untrammelled country of the Okavango's heartland, water crossings are often necessary.*

**ABOVE**  *A restored Tiger Moth flies over a herd of buffalo.*

**FOLLOWING SPREAD**  *PJ Bestelink, here watching his horses return at dusk, sits comfortably in the rarefied realm of the handful of individuals we came to know whose association with the wilds is an instinctive, canny second nature. Okavango Horse Safaris camp.*

# ELEPHANT PASSAGE

I am sailing. I hear the sound of a breaking wave, then another sweeping toward the shore. Growing loud. Clouds carried in a gentle breeze scud across the moon's face. There are pieces missing. The imperfect shape of the nearly full moon appears again. I am on deck, high in the trees.

Trees? I peer at the floating, silver-etched shapes in the darkness around me. Palm leaves, the giant forms of the trees of the Okavango. I have woken in the Okavango night, and the shimmering, now moonlit black and silver water is the deep channel that runs past Mokolwane Camp. I listen intently for what had awoken me. Hearing nothing and shivering slightly against the cold, I am driven back to the warmth of my bed.

Sleep evades me and I huddle my blanket around me and listen. It comes again. First a single splash, then a sighing of wavelets. Then a new sound, a thunderous, urgent splashing. There are no animal sounds, no calling, but something agitated is pushing through the water. It comes closer, louder and louder, the waves mount to a crescendo, fade, then grow still.

I wait for a time, that strange poised kind of waiting, where I am not certain if I stayed awake or drifted off to sleep again. Then it comes again. The sound is coming from behind the camp. I wake Peter to be certain he hears it too. The sound fills the night and we listen.

'Elephants?' I ask as the dark grows quiet. I sense Peter's nod rather than see it.

'Lots.' And then I am adrift again.

Towards dawn, from high in the jackalberries, screaming and moaning baboons wake me again. A leopard is passing through. The moon is sinking below the tree line. It has set when I wake again to the woodsmoke scent of a new dawn's campfire.

Today is the last day of our 10-day horse safari and we plan to ride to Kujwana, the base camp. It is with a sense of an adventure drawing to a close that I pull on my still-dusty jodhpurs, then my riding boots and chaps. The birds seem to know my mind is elsewhere this morning and, ignored, their cacophony grows ever louder. I smile to myself as a black-headed oriole lands on my wash stand, cocks his head and utters

his haunting, opus call. I hear the liquid pouring from a hollow jar call of the coppery-tailed coucal, the dominating chatter of the babblers, the raucous grey go-away-bird and then, above it all, what I am listening for, the soaring spirit call of the African fish-eagle.

Distracted by the birds I am late again and, running, I arrive at the outdoor breakfast spread in the shade of an ancient sycamore fig. It is a mean feat but one I have perfected over the past few days: to swallow piping-hot sweet tea, a peeled orange and a bowl of honey-roasted muesli simultaneously. Between the giant trees I watch horses, riders and grooms break the early morning rays into jets of sunlight, sprinkled with golden dust thrown up by the horses' hooves. The horses are being led to the edge of the flooded molapo for the deep-water crossing, which we must make to leave the camp island. Another group of grooms is loading the saddles and bridles, shiny with new oil, into the mokoro that will carry them to the horses on the other side.

Stripping down to my underwear and loading my gear into the mokoro with the saddles, I mount Sehube, my horse for the safari, and lead him to the water's edge. Clutching his mane, I half float-swim, half ride across the channel and, like a christening, the cool water washes over us. As his hooves leave the ground and he swims freely beneath me, I concentrate all of my being on my horse and stretch out over his arching back. Sehube takes my load and as his powerful stroke draws us to the other side, I wonder if we have swum over other, perhaps greater tracks made in the night, now vanished beneath the water.

The grooms towel Sehube dry and saddle him and I ride up to PJ Bestelink, our host and guide, who is looking down at tracks that are perfectly etched in the wet sand. There are huge tracks of elephant adults and exact miniature replicas of their babies, and he is smiling.

I can never quite explain my deep affection for elephants. It is as if long ago, before I was born, or perhaps when my soul roamed another world, that our relationship began. It is an attachment older and more powerful than I am, and I know I would be far poorer in spirit and somehow lost if elephants were not present in my world. Elephants are, too, a symbol of a wilderness without constrictive boundaries, of a wilderness intact. If these tracks we are riding over are a part of a wild

**ABOVE** *Winter breakfast. Okavango Horse Safaris.*

**OPPOSITE** *To encounter a herd of buffalo in the mist of a cool winter's pre-dawn is to give lease to our spirituality. Moremi Game Reserve.*

**FOLLOWING PAGES** *Mombo Camp and Burchell's zebra; An Abu Camp Elephant-back Safari crosses a shallow floodplain.*

breeding herd, perhaps the largest herd in Africa roaming freely under the moon, then my presence here is seeking affirmation of their existence.

This morning, tracking elephants in the usual way is rendered impossible as every island, every piece of high ground, is surrounded by water and as soon as we pick up tracks they disappear again beneath the water. It becomes a guessing, instinctive search for PJ, who has to draw on years of past experience of game movement during the flood season. We lose the tracks again and again, to stumble on them kilometres later as we criss-cross the islands in the elephants' passage.

This immense body of water is not always present here, but this is winter and the season of the Okavango's flood. The heavy rains that fall in the highlands of Angola are brought by swollen rivers to the Kalahari Desert. There is no sea or mighty river to take up the floodwaters which spread out instead across the flat desert to create a delta of incomparable magnitude. It transforms a desert into a haven of life. Aestivating frogs and fish are reborn, verdant grasses shoot through the surface of the shallows and a myriad wild things feed and proliferate. By the spring the flood is starting to dwindle and in early summer the floodwaters begin to recede and shrink into pools and deep channels. The green shallows become grasslands which must sustain the animals until midsummer when the sound of thunder and lightning patterns rip at the sky and the rainy season begins.

The floodwaters of this delta do not always flow in exactly the same course, but rather shift in response to the fault lines under this wide, flat country that lies at the foot of Africa's Great Rift Valley. This year the water is tipped by a tectonic shift to the west, where we are riding, and perhaps the elephants know this and are here seeking the first new grass.

Once again we cross the tracks of an elephant breeding herd and again we scan a horizon, empty of elephants. Now I must tear myself away from the image I have carried in my mind from my night imaginings and face the prospect that, instead of one large herd, there are actually only small splinter herds of elephants traversing the islands.

A muted whistle breaks the silence: it is Gaolape Bachae, our riflebearer and rear guard. I look in the direction in which he is pointing and PJ waves the piece of wild sage he customarily carries in acknowledgement of Gaolape's signal. In the dim light under the tall canopy of jackalberries, figs and the dark green of the mangosteens is a grey and distinctive hulk leaning against a wild date palm, asleep. We ride up as quietly and with as little movement as is possible, to stand perhaps 30 metres from him. We are downwind, yet still he stirs to wakefulness. Unaware of what has disturbed him, he slowly begins to feed. I dart a quick look around to be certain he is alone. There is only one set of tracks, his, and I am overwhelmed with guilty disappointment.

He stands now on three legs as he shakes the fruit of the wild date palm from between the fronds to fall on the ground around him. This is not an unusual stance for a mature elephant but, as he moves to feed, he drags his crooked, back leg with a slow heaviness.

Thoughts crowd through my head. This is a hunting concession. Is this elephant wounded? Could he have fallen into a hole? It is easily done as the floodwater fills hundreds of mouse, aardvark, warthog, porcupine and other holes and tunnels that would collapse under an elephant's weight. I see no scars. Is he suffering from arthritis in those enormous joints? I focus powerful binoculars on his eyes. There are no signs of pain, red streaks or lack of focus, only soft elephant eyes, but our concern seems to be communicated to him and he moves slowly and painstakingly away.

Two expansive molapos stretch ahead and we ride across them in silence. We watch spurwinged and Egyptian geese leave their busy feeding and see red-billed teal take flight, a sharp v-pattern to their wings. White-faced duck are calling. The pantomime here gradually draws me away from my sadness over the injured elephant bull when, from behind, there is a sudden crashing through the water.

There is a familiarity to the sound and I have to control myself to turn Sehube around slowly. But it is not elephants. Instead a hundred or more Burchell's zebra prance into view, completely unaware of us. They are distracted by something behind them and stop momentarily to

look back before running from the water, straight on, right into the midst of our horses. And there we stand. Riders motionless, holding our breath. Horses nonplussed, among the zebra. The zebra appear comforted by the presence of the horses and for long moments they graze side by side. Then, as suddenly, the dynamic changes and the zebra begin to run again. PJ signals and, with goose-flesh beneath my shirt and breathing hard, we race off with the zebra, a blur of black and white and dust.

All thoughts are erased from my mind, nothing exists outside of this moment. Sehube and I move as one, we fly across the earth, the sky. All the world is tumult, wind, the thud and crash of hooves on sand through water. I forget to breathe and then the zebra are gone. We slow and stop to stand alone again, with our horses blowing and pawing the ground. White foam flecks their muzzles.

It is time for a rest and chocolate and oranges, and PJ looks for a shady island with good grass for the horses. My mood has changed, my spirit lifted to another level. I do not care if we find a rest spot or not, or if we get lost, or what we see today. The sun no longer seems distant, out of reach. I feel its heat on my back. The bothersome dust is earth mingling

with the air and I savour its bitter taste on my tongue. Water and land are merged – all that matters is here and now and I am a part of it.

There is so much water here. We have to make a long detour through a series of deep channels to reach a far-off sand tongue. We squat, balanced on top of our saddles, our stirrups crossed over the top to stay dry. We wade and swish through the water for 20 minutes or more, gradually working our way to the tall canopy of trees and palms, the promise of dry land. The day is hot now and the water blue and inviting. Eventually we begin the final deep push and, dripping, we emerge onto the island. The thought of chocolate and oranges is enticing now, but, as we look for a picnic spot, Gaolape whistles through his teeth. At the same time, I look down to check my stirrups and see elephant tracks, fresh elephant tracks of all sizes.

Gaolape whistles again, more urgently, but this is unnecessary, all our eyes are fixed on the series of islands which stretch away from ours. From between the trees, elephants are materialising, grey hulks, ivory showing softly in the sun. As they move, the towering trees seem dwarfed by their size. Between them, trunks stretched forward, jockeying for attention

and space, desperate to keep up, come the babies. It is an emergence, a forest genesis of hundreds of elephants birthed by the grove of giant trees. Ancient beasts from a primal land.

PJ signals for us to move further downwind, as the elephants are massing on the edge of a very deep channel – the only path to the large sand tongue stretching away into the west. It is difficult for us to move downwind of all the elephants. More and more are appearing at the deep water's edge and their pushing through the molapo drowns out the sound of our surreptitious

progress. Again drawing on his bush-man's insight, in a flash decision PJ leads us into the protection of a young mopane thicket, where we hide behind the dense foliage with only the horses' heads protruding, perhaps 80 metres from the crossing. Signed to silence by PJ, and with reins slackened for the horses to graze, we watch and wait.

Behind us the elephants have picked up traces of our scent and have melted like grey ghosts back into the trees. I imagine they will swing round to follow the greater body of the herd.

There is a long silence and then a loud splash, like a tree fallen into the water. I turn to peer along the water's edge. Two hundred metres from us, as one cohesive elephant train, the herd begins to cross. The sound of their passage grows explosive, like thunder, and fills the morning air entirely. Elephants walk, wade and swim. The water is churned white and waves roll against the shore. Their dark wet bodies are thrown into shining relief against the bright reflection of the sun off the water. They are like heavy clouds on a low sky etched with silver.

'It was them,' I say to no one in particular. 'The sound of last night.'

At first the adults are urgency in slow motion, too serious to succumb to the playful invitations of the babies, which frolic and gambol in the water. It is a marvellous game, that of carefree babies luring careful adults into their play and today, on this river crossing of nearly 300 elephant, between Mokolwane and Kujwana islands in the heart of the Okavango Delta, the cautious adults pause and for a time give in to the infectious spirit of the crossing.

PJ leads us out of the trees to edge a little closer, and we are privileged to 20 exquisite minutes of the secret world of the elephant.

Finally, the grand scene trickles to a close and, straining to hear the last sounds of the departing elephants,

I lead Sehube to the water to drink, but he stands stubbornly, sniffing the air. All of the elephants have crossed so this is strange behaviour. I stroke Sehube's neck and talk softly to him but he pulls away and I notice all the horses are straining against their reins to leave. We turn as a group in the direction of what seems to be alarming the horses when three young bulls, stragglers of the herd, step out of the trees and approach the crossing point where we are standing.

We are no longer hidden but in full view and in the direct path of their crossing. The leading bull sees us and throws his head, shaking dust from his ears, then raises his trunk to try to find our scent. I turn my face to the wind but the air is still. The elephant, uncertain, begins a slow charge, and PJ signals for us to go. I turn Sehube and, in a walk-trot, we move away. Sehube strains against my hold but to run will incite the elephants. I keep Sehube's head pointed away, but I watch the elephant. In spite of the wet terrain, mud and dust are thrown up by the heavy gait of his charge and he moves with frightening, unprecedented speed.

We are all nearly back into the security of the mopane island when PJ turns to face the elephant. Peter is right behind him. The elephant stops abruptly, lifts his trunk again to scent the air and, in a change of heart, turns back to the other two bulls. PJ signals for us to move slowly back towards the bulls. To our surprise, he comes again, this time faster and more determined and, in a scatter of hooves, we have our horses back within the island. My heart is thundering in my chest, yet I am strangely light and in control. For the second time today, nothing exists outside the moment, the here and now; the elephant, my horse and me on earth under a close, blue sky.

Thwarted by the trees, the young bull turns from his charge to race across the channel instead. The other two bulls follow immediately, but the channel is deep and the going cumbersome and one young bull falls in a hole. He tries to right himself, in a 'hoping we did not notice', clumsy flourish. We giggle then laugh out loud as the tension flows away.

On the far side the elephants vanish, swallowed up once again by the cool green and grey of the forest. I lean forward on my horse's neck, put my arms around him and bury my face in his mane. It smells of sweat and earth and horse and water, of oiled leather and dry grass and sun – of today, of now.

**TOP** *Abu Camp elephants curiously follow a brave young visitor.*

**ABOVE** *Red lechwe rams on a misty floodplain.*

*It is one of the most difficult challenges, when standing before a wild country in a natural state, to accept death. Death often seems tragic and is frequently protracted and cruel and, when emotional distress screams at one to take a hand, I remind myself that I have yet to see a wild animal in Africa die of old age.*

**ABOVE**  *Recently Lake Ngami, to the south of the Okavango Delta, flooded for the first time in 30 years. The water drew millions of sparrow-sized red-billed quelea to new feeding grounds. Each day their numbers swelled until the air grew thick with their living clouds.*

**OPPOSITE, ABOVE**  *A warm summer shower brings brollies and bare feet onto the wooden bridge over the deep, perennial Xigera Channel.*

**OPPOSITE, BELOW**  *White rhinoceros were re-introduced into the Delta in the past decade and remain a rare sight. Mombo.*

**ABOVE** *Emblematic bird of the Delta, the African fish-eagle, with its prey. Nxamaseri Channel.*

**OPPOSITE, ABOVE** *Moonrise. Nxamaseri Channel, Okavango River.*

**OPPOSITE, BELOW** *The world seen through the veil of a fine net can hold the quality of dreams. Chitabe Trails Camp.*

**ABOVE**  *Two lions subdue an impala ewe. Mombo, Chief's Island.*

**OPPOSITE**  *Spotted hyaena. Moremi Game Reserve.*

**FOLLOWING SPREAD**  *The full moon reflected in the Okavango Delta.*

# CHOBE, LINYANTI & SAVUTI

I did not see it coming until it was too late. Beverly, with a woman's intuition, had scampered, dusted her heels at the first signs, but I was too slow, naively unaware that I was being stalked. Even when she had me cornered, I did not realise that I was the target. It was masterful, considered and flawlessly executed.

'Outrageous,' the woman muttered almost to herself as she took a fresh cup and waited for me to finish pouring myself an outsize mug of the freshly brewed coffee. I might have ignored it, as I had been up since before the dawn more than five hours ago and the coffee had my attention. 'I was sold 50 000 elephants,' she said, passing me the milk and holding the sugar bowl open for me to help myself.

'Fifty thousand! Huh!' she exclaimed. She was looking down but she had me now and although the words were innocent enough, if somewhat exasperated, it was the voice, the way she uttered them that made them ugly, sharp.

I looked out to where the water dripped from the lodge veranda eaves. The day was grey and soft. A fine rain was falling and was drawn like a gossamer gauze over the land. It gathered on the tips of the leaves and trembled there until it fell. The frogs were celebrating, their voices a delicate crystal wind-chime orchestra. The water in the Zibadianja Lagoon lay in smooth, silver-grey sheets between the papyrus beds. The long thin leaves of the reeds had all been bent in one direction by the wind in the night and, black now against the water, they had the clean crisp symmetry of a stylised Japanese bamboo painting. A herd of lechwe stood still in the shallows, hunched with their backs toward the rain. Collared pratincoles flew like darts with their curved wings, hawking insects low over the water. It was an Africa I loved but there would be no elephant here. The rain that had begun falling two days ago had put paid to that. There may be a few lone bulls perhaps, but the tumultuous, trumpeting ranks of the breeding herds that she had been told about, that came in their thousands to the Linyanti and the Chobe, forced by their thirst to the only place of water in the dry season, would be gone. So too would the gathering of bulls, which

stand patiently about the waterhole of Savuti, waiting for their place in the hierarchy to drink, be dispersed.

They would be gone into the vast savanna and mopane forest interior of the Chobe National Park. Gone into a quiet wilderness, far from the press of tourists that parade the narrow margin between the red sand hills and the Chobe River. Gone into a trackless country where they navigated by memory to rainwater pans in slippery black clay. Gone to secret, still places with plentiful food. Places where they could drink alone and their babies could roll and tussle in the delicious warm, dark mud.

I wanted to tell her that. I wanted to tell her, as she sneered at the coffee she had poured and tipped it out over the wall, that she could go there, to the interior, and wait by a pan. That if she were lucky they would come, not 50 000, but a few, quietly through the trees, like ghosts. Sniffing the air with their trunks, cautious, the babies touching their mothers for reassurance. The teenagers with their ears flared wide, full of bravado in the face of imaginary danger but with the tips of their trunks in their mouths, a security for their immature uncertainty. I wanted to tell her that if she were lucky there would be kudu too and warthog or perhaps even a roan or a sable, with its regal, swept-back horns.

But she did not want my stories or ideas, she wanted to add me to the consensus she was trying to garner that this was not the Africa she had been sold by her travel agent, the perfect world she had in her head. She wanted to add my voice to the growing petition of her complaint. And as I took a breath to speak, she dropped her voice into a conspiratorial whisper. The voice she used now was soft, intimate and even though I could not hear the words, I could detect in their tone traces of hemlock. Almost, ever so nearly, did I fall into her trap.

I had caught her husband's eye. It brimmed with weariness and was sad and I sensed a weight upon his limbs, as if he was dragging his being even though he sat still. It had stopped me leaning forward out of politeness to hear her whisper, prevented my being cajoled into her confidence. He sat with their son on a couch, reviewing the pictures they had made. The boy sat close beside the

**ABOVE** *Great white egrets fishing.*

**OPPOSITE** *The still, deep waters of the Chobe River are an ideal place for hot, thirsty elephants to drink, swim and play.*

big fish broke away. I remember elephants or a hippopotamus in our camp and my mother with a dishcloth, terrified, but too excited to run away. I remember a huge ugly catfish flapping wildly in the bottom of the boat and a flight of white birds behind my father's head and the faraway look on his face as we puttered slowly home, navigating close to the bank, almost beneath the trees.

Perhaps I should have told her that or of the other things one does not forget. Camping at night at Nogatsaa, a pan deep in the Chobe National Park, beneath a full moon with friends. And the lions coming down to drink and then sauntering up to our camp and lying down and roaring and roaring and then falling asleep. Or another story I put to paper not far from here on a stifling hot spring day, describing how a dying elephant's breath had touched my leg. Writing and writing as the tears flowed down my cheeks. I wanted to tell her about Lloyd Wilmot sitting in the middle of a muddy, fetid pan in Savuti, sipping a cold drink whilst the old elephant bulls stood around on three legs waiting for him to leave.

I should have, but her voice was trailing off. I was being rude. 'You're the author,' she said, putting her hand on my arm. But I had not heard the question.

I do not have the gift of the gab, I am no good at witty repartee and so I said nothing and, as gently as I could, lifted her hand from my arm and walked out onto the veranda, out into the soft summer rain. Rain that had set in motion more things than you can say.

man concentrating on the camera, his arm lay loosely across his father's thigh. He was excited, pointing at details, looking up every now and then into his father's face.

I wanted to escape. She was complaining about her guide. The lions he had tracked were a paltry four, asleep beneath the trees. 'Family,' I thought, as I looked into her eyes, but it was a mistake and, encouraged, she grew more vehement still. I looked away.

I had first come here with my family sometime in the late 1960s. My father had dragged a caravan, a wife and three pre-teenage boys up here. What stamina and resolve my parents must have had. I wish I could remember more, for that sort of epic does not come about without love and tolerance and things given and shared.

I remember setting out in our tiny dinghy, the gunwales as low as a dugout canoe, to catch tigerfish in the rapids where the Chobe River joins the Zambezi. I see the copper lure bouncing over the surface as we trolled and I can feel the anguish in my heart when my first

**LEFT** *Chobe Game Lodge, where Richard Burton and Elizabeth Taylor married for the second time.*

**OPPOSITE, ABOVE** *Wild dogs with impala kill.*

**OPPOSITE, BELOW** *A black kite swoops on a dove that landed in deep water.*

**PREVIOUS SPREAD**  *In the vast sweep of the dry country of Savuti, only a few pans provide permanent water and elephant bulls linger there. Chobe National Park.*

**ABOVE**  *Lightning strikes around Savuti Camp.*

**LEFT**  *A young bull throws his trunk and flares his ears in a threat display. Chobe River.*

**ABOVE**  *A crocodile tears the flesh from a hippopotamus carcass. Chobe River.*

**OPPOSITE, ABOVE**  *Hippopotamus charge. Linyanti Channel.*

**OPPOSITE, BELOW LEFT**  *Storm clouds gathering. Savuti.*

**OPPOSITE, BELOW RIGHT**  *A bat-eared fox emerges from its burrow at dusk.*

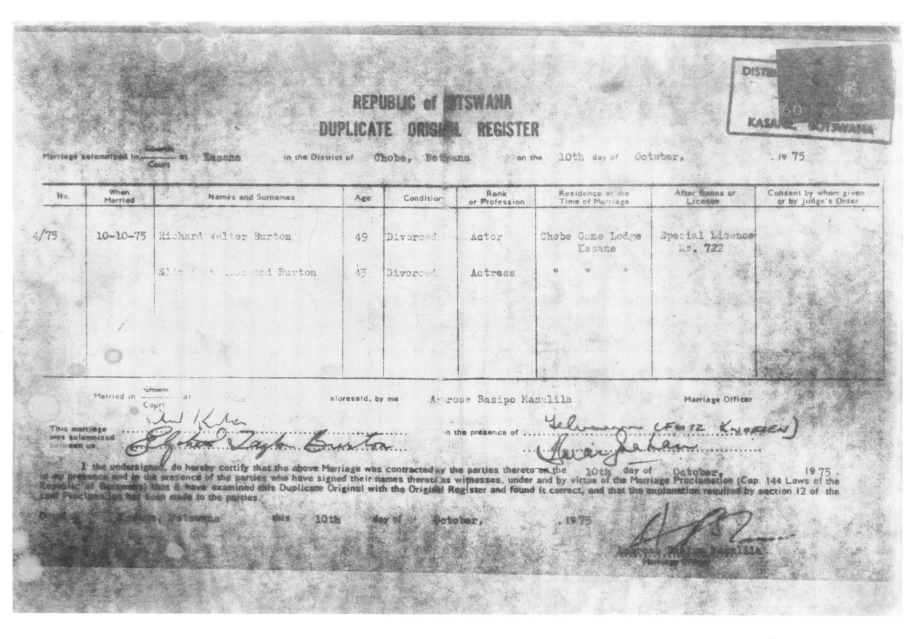

**REPUBLIC of BOTSWANA**

**DUPLICATE ORIGINAL REGISTER**

Marriage solemnized in ——— at Kasane    in the District of    Chobe, Botswana    on the 10th day of October,    19 75

| No. | When Married | Names and Surnames | Age | Condition | Rank or Profession | Residence at the Time of Marriage | After Banns or Licence | Consent by whom given or by Judge's Order |
|---|---|---|---|---|---|---|---|---|
| 4/75 | 10-10-75 | Richard Walter Burton | 49 | Divorced | Actor | Chobe Game Lodge Kasane | Special Licence No. 722 | |
| | | Elizabeth Rosemond Burton | 43 | Divorced | Actress | " " " | | |

Married in ——— at ——— aforesaid, by me    Ambrose Basipo Masalila    Marriage Officer

This marriage was solemnized between us ——— *Elizabeth Taylor Burton* ———    in the presence of ——— Selwanga (Fritz Knudsen) ———

I the undersigned, do hereby certify that the above Marriage was contracted by the parties thereto on the 10th day of October, 19 75 in my presence and in the presence of the parties who have signed their names thereto as witnesses, under and by virtue of the Marriage Proclamation (Cap. 144 Laws of the Republic of Botswana) that I have examined this Duplicate Original with the Original Register and found it correct, and that the explanation required by section 12 of the said Proclamation has been made to the parties.

Dated at Kasane, Botswana    this    10th    day of    October,    19 75

Ambrose Basipo Masalila
Marriage Officer

**ABOVE** *Richard Burton and Elizabeth Taylor's highly publicised second marriage at Chobe Game Lodge was in essence a quiet affair, without guests, presided over by the lodge management and the Magistrate of Kasane.*

**ABOVE & LEFT** *It is not the physical size of lions but their eyes, hot with cold fury and contempt, that make hearts shiver and turn away.*

**FOLLOWING SPREAD** *Monika Seanokeng relaxes in the tented luxury of a King's Pool suite. Linyanti.*

**PREVIOUS SPREAD, & ABOVE & OPPOSITE, ABOVE** *Elephants are frequently cited as a favourite African animal and there is no more engaging time to be among them than in the presence of water or a mud wallow, when even herd-leading adults abandon their usually sombre demeanour to indulge in the luxury.*

**LEFT** *A heavily fed spotted hyaena snaps at vultures encroaching on a carcass. Duma Tau area, Linyanti.*

**OPPOSITE, BELOW** *A crocodile's intention is more clearly understood than that of a mouth-agape young hippopotamus in approaching the floating body of a young bull killed in a fight. Chobe National Park.*

**FOLLOWING SPREAD** *I fondly recall the dry season in Savuti, when elephant bulls gather at the pans to wait their turn to drink. Doves flutter about, landing on the domed grey backs and tree-trunk sized feet to sip at the puddles that the elephant have spilled. Feeling them there, the elephant keep their feet still until the doves have drunk. It is a memory warm with contentment, in the shadow of awe, when I saw for a moment how the world could be, when to exercise one's might is to be considerate of doves.*

# ZIMBABWE

## MANA POOLS & THE ZAMBEZI

**PAGE 142** *In the hot basin of the Zambezi River, winterthorn trees grow thick and tall on the flat reaches of the floodplains, and buffalo come especially to eat the seed pods that have fallen there.*

**PAGES 144/145** *In the vicinity of villages, elephants cross at night to feed on the reeded sandbars.*

**TOP** *In the presence of wild dogs, impala flee with a strange high-jumping, rocking horse-like gait.*

**ABOVE** *Wild dogs mob a hyaena that might otherwise steal their kill.*

**OPPOSITE** *The floodplains of the Zambezi provide sweet grass and scant cover for predators.*

# Mana Pools & The Zambezi

History records David Livingstone as being frustrated by the Zambezi River. It claims that he had dreams for it as a route of commerce, a path by which to open up the African interior. His plans were foiled by Victoria Falls, the Kariba Gorge and the Cahora Bassa Gorge. But what a grand foiling. Too grand for frustration. I imagine it was more a wonder, an exaltation, a transport by this artery of the African heartland.

He was, after all, a compulsive explorer. He did not hunt game in excessive quantities nor did he bully or make war. He had been given an imposing brief by a faraway authority, but he was driven in his day to day to look beyond the horizon and behind the mountain.

The excitement of one's first passage through new country, I have it in me too, the coercion by the pulse of the land to know more. To this end, the Zambezi is not in the least a frustration. It reaches instead to a satisfaction, a power to still us, to mesmerise.

I walked out from our camp one morning at Mana Pools. The air was warm and I walked slowly, trailing my hands across the bulbous swellings of the sturdy bases of winterthorn trees. They form a tall forest here on the flat floodplain banks of the Zambezi River, but their trunks are widespread and mostly straight, without branches or leaves, and one can see between them. I was walking towards a lone elephant bull without haste, pausing to feel with my skin and my hair for the stirrings of the breeze. I altered my course every now and then, staying downwind. A squirrel 'chick-chirred' an alarm at my presence and I saw him high on a trunk, holding flat against the yellowed bark with his head pointing down and his tail twitching each time he chirred. A thought popped into my head and I chuckled, 'Did ya ever eat a squirrel?' It was a private joke that I had with an American friend, and it had nothing to do with squirrels, it was about fishing.

He would have liked it here, my American friend, doing this, but his wife may have been afraid. Pity. Maybe he would come alone. It was the kind of place you could be alone with just some friends. I am glad my wife is my friend. You should tell her that, I thought.

I paused before some open ground and then, keeping a termite mound between me and the elephant, I moved forward

again. A bit more quickly now. The base of the termite mound was broad, as wide as a car, with a high step before tapering to its lopsided top a metre or so above my head. Cautiously I moved around. There was a natural seat near the top and, crawling up on all fours, I dusted the thorns from it and settled down.

All the while I had kept half an eye on the elephant, looking out sideways from under my brows. Funny that, how you feel a direct look will expose you, reveal your being there or your intent. I have seen my dog do it on the beach, trotting back and forth sniffing at nothing, with her eyes to the ground and all the while trying to work around behind another hound. The elephant ignored me. He was picking up fallen seed pods one by one. I could hear them crack and split as he bit down.

The trees grew right up to the edge of the riverbank here and, from the elevated position of the termite mound, I could see down into the water where a giant tree had fallen in. Its roots had torn a gap in the bank and the hippopotamus had made a path out of the river there, turning it in time into a gully. It was lined on its sides with the dry splattering of their dung.

I had brought my notes: how long, how wide, how big, when it rains, dates, and my notebook to write, but in the conjuring of those ideas my thoughts grew listless, sluggish and died, faltering on their blandness

before they had begun. A giant kingfisher swooped in onto an exposed root of the fallen tree and twitched his tail, distracting me. Suddenly his feathers all went tight, flat against his sides. He cocked his head at the water. I could not see the fish but his head jerked again, watching it. He strained forward, leaning from his perch, poised. I counted, going, going, but he pulled back at the last, ruffling his wings loose. I felt like him in my mind. Poised, taut, ready to begin, but that silvery thought just would not come.

A hippopotamus snorted out in the river. I looked up to see it, but the sun was on the water and, in the riffle of the wind, the bright light shattered into myriad facets, too sharp to look at. It was reflected up under the trees, onto the elephant, onto me. I squinted and was about to look away when I saw it. The river. The river, you fool. The river was all of it. The river was what it was, the core, the epitome, all of it drawn together. A river runs through it. The Zambezi River.

Norman Maclean's words. I sat on a termite mound beside an elephant in a hot African valley and tried to remember them. 'Eventually, all things merge into one, and a river runs through it. The river was cut by the world's great flood and runs over rocks from the basement of time. On some of the rocks are timeless raindrops. Under the rocks are the words, and some of the words are theirs.'

The words of the buffalo, the bold poems of the elephants, the songs of the birds, the searing chorus of fire, the litany of drought, the sly whispering of the crocodiles and the hippopotamus snort that Livingstone heard and so did I. All these turned in the sand and drifted down past the tiger fish and the barbel. They snared themselves on the fallen trees, in the nets of the fishermen in their dugout canoes, impaled themselves on the arrows of the hunters and their spears. And the river took back what it had given, but some words were left beneath the stones. And, with time, these soft tracings etched themselves layer upon layer into the rock, an epitaph that finally made them theirs.

I could see the words of history clearly from where I sat, the passages from time, indelible upon the land. To the north, the sharp rise of the hills softened by a grey-blue haze. Beneath the canopy of the winterthorns I had only glimpses of the sky, except at the horizon where

it joined the narrow distance of the river, robin's egg blue, turning white. The river, through the trees, brown and blue and wide. It turned towards me and then away, back towards the hills. A hundred scattered sandbars, the almond shape of eyes, some just a suggestion beneath the current, others standing clear, a bleached yellow in the sun. The current riffling though the shallows, roiling, greasy smooth in the deeper runs. The long finger of an island towards the far side with a stand of tall green reeds on its downstream end and a dense forest. A regiment of straight clean trunks lining the near side. Small in the distance a hippopotamus plodded, splashing through the middle river.

It was hot as I walked back to camp, boding an afternoon of dark black clouds and thunder.

'What did you find?'

'Nothing much,' and I picked up a glass of water from the ground and drank it all and then held the glass up high and, opening my mouth, let the last few drops fall down on my tongue. A bushbuck barked, but when I turned around it was gone.

THIS PAGE, CENTRE *Guests on the deck of Chikwenya Camp;* RIGHT *A vine remains long after the it tree has climbed has died.*

OPPOSITE, TOP RIGHT *Members of the Senzangakhona Primary School outing to Victoria Falls.*

*As I stood at the foot of the bank beneath
this elephant and watched, I felt neither
bigger nor smaller, I felt a part. And in
that place, where I felt not dominion but
a belonging, there took seed in me a sense
that I wanted to hold and cherish.
It coursed in me and, holding myself still,
I let it come until I felt its warmth through
all of me, until it was bigger than everything else, too big to last. I was glad of
it and for the time it stayed, for something
of it lingers in me still.*

**TOP**  *The solitary buffalo bulls that wander the edge of the river are notoriously disdainful of human presence.*

**ABOVE**  *During the dry season, lone elephant bulls feed on rafts of water weed in the Zambezi.*

**OPPOSITE**  *Victoria Falls Gorge.*

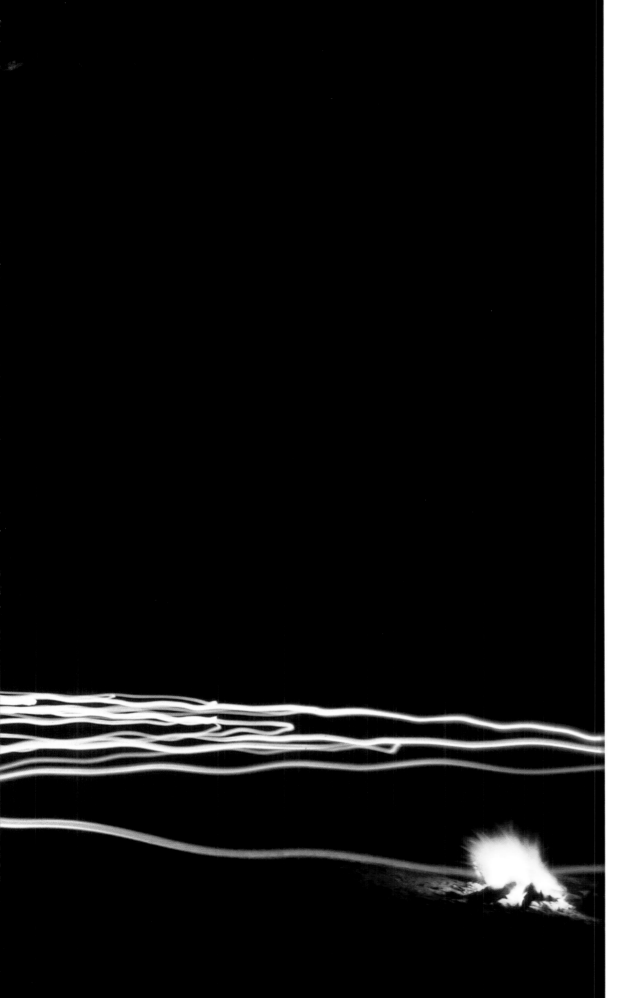

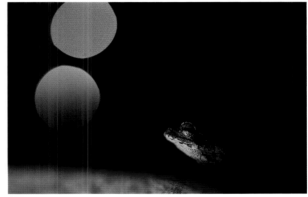

**CLOCKWISE FROM LEFT** *Dinner beneath a baobab; al fresco bathroom; foam-nest frog; last light on the Zambezi and dinner setting. Chikwenya Camp, Mana Pools.*

# NO COMFORT

Through the shimmer of heat rising from the unshaded land, I am watching a blue ripple made by the wind as it courses over the wide swathe of the Zambezi River. Beside a submerged sandbar, where the water rises in a light chop, I can make out the rounded backs of hippopotamus. Occasionally a short, whale-like spray rises from their midst and then, a second later, delayed by the distance, I hear their booming contact snort.

The floodplain between me and the river is little more than a low, wide sandbar, pockmarked with the passage of now absent game and fringed along the water's edge with a brocade of green that has been cropped as closely as a manicured lawn. A single baboon squats on its haunches a few metres from the shore, rooting disinterestedly in the lethargy of the heat. Beside the mouth of a short, shallow inlet, the ridged back of a broad-girthed crocodile lies half in, half out of the transition between the water and the land.

I have been talking to Lloyd Mashuri beneath the deep shade of the giant riverine sausage trees that cluster the bank of this unmistakably African river. He is gone now and I find myself lost in thought at the story I have just heard. I catch myself in my reverie, staring fixedly past the low sandbars and on to the high, blue hills of Zambia that rise behind the indigenous forest of the distant shore.

A legion of towering cumulus heads is massing above the heights of the hills, taunting the hot, blue land and, along a distant ridge, smoke from an unseen wildfire is absorbed into the steely sheen of the sky. It was on a day much like this that Lloyd set off past these same hills on a canoe safari. It was a small safari, just himself and a young honeymoon couple from Norway in two canoes, who pushed off from the bank into a calm dawn that lay in perfect reflection upon the water.

The current turned the noses of the Indian canoes downstream, drawing them quietly, but deceptively quickly, past the bank. Only occasionally did the dip and splash of the paddles fragment the reflected sky.

It was a fine morning and their conversation was comfortable, but sporadic, as they sat captivated by the vista of the river and the occasional interest of the passing bank. A darter perched high on an exposed root, ducked its head at their approach, poised itself for flight and then thought better of it and, with a quick snake-like movement of its head, watched them pass close beneath.

Lloyd was alone in his canoe. It sat lower in the water than that of his clients, loaded with much of the camping and cooking equipment for the safari. It made the canoe more sluggish in the water, more susceptible to the currents and eddies around the sandbars and fallen logs, but Lloyd was used to it and steered the craft with the economy of a professional.

Coming to a place where the bank ended and the river made a dog-leg to the right, Lloyd swung the nose of his canoe upstream to compensate for the push of the main river ahead, and his canoe swung in a perfect arc to face downstream. Behind him the Norwegian couple completely botched the manoeuvre and, after being spun around by the eddy, they were left facing upstream, drifting backwards down the river.

Lloyd heard them giggling behind him and he smiled. Theirs would be a good marriage, he thought to himself, for there is little more testing on a couple's compatibility and tolerance than learning to paddle a rudderless canoe together.

The bank beside which they had been paddling had given way to a wide floodplain that rose in a series of stepped banks until it reached the high ground with its distinctive albida forests. Even at this distance Lloyd could make out the park-like quality of the forest, its virtually continuous canopy held almost 10 metres clear of the ground on the thick, bowled, leaning trunks of the trees. On the floodplain, a herd of 60 or so impala grazed on short grass.

Lloyd was looking ahead, planning his route between the sandbars, trying to discern the shifting channels, when he saw the first of a herd of elephant enter the river from a long island, which divided the river at this point. It would be exciting to drift down among them, he thought, for, if it is handled correctly, a canoe's approach is almost silent and from the water one can get much closer than on the land. The young couple had, however, voiced their reservation at close encounters and so Lloyd let his canoe drift downstream for a minute more and then drew the canoes up on a sandbar that stood a few inches proud of the water. A heron

**OPPOSITE** *The park-like quality of Mana Pools, with its flat country and mature uncluttered forest, is divested of this illusion by the tension inherent in its game, the nervous awareness necessary for survival, the apprehension of death in the living.*

that had been fishing there took off with a croak of annoyance and, with heavy, languid wingbeats and its feet and neck stretched out, it flew slowly downstream towards the elephants.

To their left, the mountains of the Zambian escarpment rose warm in the morning light, their folds alternating green and grey, with black in the shadows. Just above the horizon, a scattered armada of billowing white clouds was edging towards them. The elephants, 150 metres downstream, were crossing in a single file. The surface of the riverbed was surprisingly uneven and sometimes the elephants were splashing through shallows, while at others only the backs and raised tips of the trunks of the adults were visible, with the babies swimming beside them. The black wet bodies of the elephants gleamed in the light and above their backs the broad course of the river

channel passed quite close to a pod of hippopotamus that were sleeping in the shallows at the tail of a long sandbar. The water of the channel was deep, however, and Lloyd was confident that they would be safe.

A hundred or so metres upstream of the hippopotamus, something struck Lloyd a stunning blow at the base of his neck. His senses reeled, bright stars of light popping in his eyes as he fought for his balance. He felt his senses dim and, down a long tunnel, he heard a woman's hysterical scream echoing, and then he was in the water.

The cool, sharp contact of the water stopped the slip of his consciousness, although his mind remained fuzzy for those first few seconds. The screaming had stopped. The water was almost dark. He could taste the

tapered through hues of brown, green and blue, towards the horizon.

Lloyd sat astride the stern of his canoe, his feet bare on the damp sand; this was wild Africa, as good as it gets. He felt like the first man.

In silence the three of them looked on until the elephants had crossed the river and the floodplain and had disappeared into the trees, then they paddled across to the island the elephants had left and, over an open fire, Lloyd cooked breakfast. It was one of those special breakfasts that stay with you for a long time, of eggs and sausage and toast, and scalding tea sweet with condensed milk, all of which were permeated with the distinctive flavour of wood smoke.

After breakfast they slid the canoes into the muddy brown current of the Zambezi once more. Lloyd had noted where the deep channels were from the elephants' crossing and he headed for these. At one point the

familiar flavour of the Zambezi in his mouth. Something was bumping against his back and his legs.

As his focus returned, he realised that his inert body was being pulled down and across the current. 'Croc!' burst into his mind and charged like lightning through his body. He lashed out violently for the surface. The crocodile reacted instantly, shaking him like a terrier delivering the death-bite to a mouse and dragging him down. It was then that Lloyd realised that the crocodile had a hold of his shirt and not of him. He twisted, pulled and kicked out with his legs and the crocodile fought back harder, shaking him with determined, violent swipes of its head from side to side. With one of his flailing arms Lloyd caught hold of the crocodile and, spurred to extraordinary strength by adrenalin, twisted himself bodily around so that he was facing his aggressor. The

**ABOVE**  *Meves's starlings bathing.*

**OPPOSITE, MIDDLE**  *Nyala doe;* **OPPOSITE, BOTTOM**  *Young hippopotamus test their strength. Zambezi River.*

**FOLLOWING SPREAD**  *The Zambezi basin, Mana Pools.*

crocodile maintained its vice-like grip on the back of his shirt so that Lloyd was now pressed up against the underside of its jaw, its long snout lying against his own jaw and his ear, so that each time it shook him it beat him on the side of his head. Unthinkingly, Lloyd clasped its jaws against his chest, encircling them with his arms. He then brought his legs up and, joining them scissor-like behind the croc's back, he began to squeeze. The crocodile shook its head more violently and twisted, rolling in the water. Lloyd's grip stayed in place and he squeezed harder. The crocodile stopped spinning and Lloyd, his mind screaming from the shock, the effort and a desperate need for air, clamped down on the beast with the huge demonic will that comes with the last grip on the threshold of life. The crocodile hesitated, Lloyd arched his back into the effort and, nearly 30 seconds after he had been dragged down, Lloyd exploded through the surface.

The girl's screaming assaulted his senses and he looked towards them, but they were 80 metres upriver, too far away to help. His own canoe was drifting upside down about 30 metres downstream, a cool box floating lopsidedly alongside it. The hippopotamus, however, spooked by the commotion, had taken refuge in the deep water around it. Lloyd could not swim through them and the current was carrying him towards them. Looking about Lloyd saw the riffle of a barely submerged sandbar about 30 metres away, towards the middle of the river, and, hesitating only briefly, he set out on the longest swim of his life.

Halfway there he stopped to check behind him. Something bumped against his foot and he jerked it up, gasping a lungful of air.

Simultaneously he touched it again with his leg and his hand and realised, weeping with relief, that it was a sandbar. He stood up and, wading across it, found its shallowest point, but was still standing knee-deep in murky water. He shouted to the couple to come and fetch him, but the girl was hysterical, and the canoe drifted in erratic circles as her husband floundered between calming her and paddling, and then Lloyd saw the crocodile again.

It had not given up. It had surfaced about 25 metres downstream from him and was swimming determinedly towards him, a small wake spreading out from its snout. Lloyd screamed at the Norwegians to get him now. The crocodile started to speed up and it was then, staring at the closing horrific apparition, that Lloyd remembered the revolver he had uncustomarily strapped to his hip during the early hours of the dawn when he had heard a lion close to their camp.

In his fumbling hands the first shot was wild, but its explosion brought focus to his nerves and at 10 metres two shots ripped into the water where the crocodile, now slightly submerged, was starting its charge. There was a huge swirl and splash, and then nothing but the smooth surface of the river, the warm sun and a flight of birds that the gunfire had frightened into the air above the trees.

I was surprised that Lloyd did not hang onto that shirt; he burnt it that night in the camp fire.

'It had a big hole in it, Pete,' he had said, grinning broadly as we looked out from under the shade of the trees toward the river.

# ZAMBIA

## North & South Luangwa

# NORTH & SOUTH LUANGWA

Delville Wood is not a name many remember today. But I remember it. World War I. I remember it through my grandfather. He was there. He had found me looking in the tin box with his medals in it. Lightly his fingers had touched the ribbon on my hand. 'Delville Wood,' he had said, and then repeated it. 'Ranks of us in. Only a handful out,' and then he had walked outside and grasped the rail of the small veranda and stood still for a long time, looking out towards the trees.

I recall, too, sitting beside his gaunt, stiff frame during a Christmas service with all the family. The priest was reading from Psalm 23 and I noticed my grandfather's hands clasping and releasing the pressed grey flannel of his trousers. He dropped his hymn book. I picked it up and gave it back. 'Pops? What's the matter, Pops?'

Leaning forward, he had whispered in my ear, 'When you walk through the valley of the shadow of death, you fear every evil.' I knew it was something to do with the box of medals, with Delville Wood, and when I put my hand on his I could feel it shaking before he pulled away.

Delville Wood, Psalm 23, my grandfather – I thought about all of them in this valley of Africa, this valley that is the last tailings, the final throes of Africa's Great Rift Valley, the Luangwa Valley. The valley that has in its time been the valley of the shadow of death. This valley, however, did not boom and roar and split asunder amidst volleys of the mortars and the field guns, this was a quieter, more stealthy war. A creeping war, under cover of darkness, a single shot or at most a curt ripple of automatic fire echoing off the hills, its sudden, cold, harsh intrusion magnified by the silence. Mostly it was the animals that died. The elephant, the buffalo, the hippopotamus, for their meat, for the white gold that is their teeth. Death for profit, not for principle – when you pick at it, turn it over, dig a little deeper, there is nothing in it but for hunger that does not reek. Death for greed.

The persecution of the elephants of this valley began before the days of guns, with the arrival of the first Arab traders. By the late 19th century the slaughter of the elephant and the hippopotamus of Luangwa Valley was so extensive that the administrator of the territory at the time placed a ban on all hunting in the valley. By 1911 the population of elephant had re-established itself to the point where they were encroaching once more on tilled land. Under pressure, a few permits were issued for the control of these problem animals. A guidebook I have discusses this issue and concludes its consequence in a most African way – pragmatic, uninflamed, forthright. 'But the temptation to shoot the biggest ones for their tusks was too great,' it says.

Respite finally came in 1938 when the North and South Luangwa Parks were proclaimed. Bert Schultz and Norman Carr were appointed as the first game rangers. For Carr, the Luangwa was to become a life-long obsession. He became its champion, and the Luangwa Valley's

almost pristine existence today is due largely to his vigilance and effort. In the early 1950s, Carr persuaded his friend Chief Nsefu to designate some of his tribal land to be used for photographic safaris in return for the revenue being given to Chief Nsefu's community. The Nsefu Sector, with its intricate system of lagoons, mature forest and wide plains, the only portion of the park on the eastern bank of the Luangwa River, was incorporated into the South Luangwa Park in 1972, and the community is still deriving the benefit of its utilisation today.

**PAGE 162** *With their habit of laying their heads on their neighbour's rump, the vast pods of hippopotamus in the Luangwa River appear from above as molecules in a chain.*

**PAGES 164/165** *A matriarch and her two calves cross the Luangwa River. South Luangwa National Park.*

**PAGES 166/167** *The Lubanga River. North Luangwa National Park.*

Both the North and South Luangwa Parks occupy the country from the west bank of the Luangwa River through to the Muchinga Escarpment, which rises dramatically a thousand metres above the valley floor, some 50 kilometres to the west. The two parks are separated by the Munyamadzi Game Management Area, a community-based area traditionally utilised for hunting in Zambia.

Hunting legally, hunting illegally – the Luangwa Valley has had its share of guns. It is a hot valley even in winter, the river sluggish brown, with sheer tall banks of earth that crash into the water from time to time, eaten away from underneath. The splash sends the crocodiles scurrying from their warm lounging on the sand and causes the dense rafts of hippopotamus, lying head to tail, head to tail, to start and snort and the bulls to whirl around. The same guide-book claims, 'Today there is an over abundance of hippopotamus along the Luangwa River!' What does it mean by that? Just a fact? I have flown the length of the Luangwa River and there are places where the hippopotamus are many, but more where they are few. 'An over abundance.' I sense in it a more sinister overture, a righteous equivocation, a precursor to a new season of guns.

It was the rhinoceros that succumbed in the last. Gone. Their dismembered heads sold to faraway bidders. And the elephants fell, too, until the last of them took to the hills of the escarpment. They learnt to be quiet and walk on stony ground, to keep their grey shadows within the trees and to approach water with caution. To drink from small streams in the darkest hour and to hush their babies to silence and stand still and listen and listen again, ready to run. Over the great plains of the valley, the thickets of the bushveld trees and the quiet of the riverine forests, the veil of the shadow of death was hung by mercenaries of a one-sided war. Finally, the beleaguered, thin ranks of the protectors took arms themselves and the valley entered its darkest hour, and men sought each other over the barrels of their guns.

**PREVIOUS SPREAD** *The spotter plane and some of the staff, trained and supported by the Frankfurt Zoological Society. North Luangwa National Park.*

**THIS SPREAD** *Control room and camp scenes. North Luangwa National Park.*

It is one of Africa's most unsung triumphs that, that dark season has passed. It is the power of a single idea that is right. The victory of community over greed. The triumph of consideration and co-operation over distrust, the power of dialogue over force. I felt it most one warm dawn as I lay on my belly high above the still, brown river, my camera focused on the crocodiles emerging on the sand bar below. The hand-held radio by my side crackled intrusively into my concentration. 'Control. Control. Luangwa one.' Hugo van der Westhuizen's voice was muffled, scattered by the roar of the aircraft's engine, the buffeting of the wind through the open door of the spotter plane he flew. He was calling on the open frequency, everyone could hear, all the patrols, all the vehicles, all the guard posts, the scouts looking out over the valley from the tops of the hills. 'Just confirming,' but the voice trailed off. 'Confirming,' he came back, and I realised that his voice was thick, his throat tight with what he had to say. 'Confirming the birth of a black rhino. Positive...' but his voice failed him.

I rolled on my back and, putting my hands behind my head, looked at the sky. I was smiling. Hugo's choked announcement was the first recorded rhinoceros birth in the North Luangwa in nearly 30 years, the culmination of nearly 16 years' commitment to North Luangwa and its attendant communities by the Frankfurt Zoological Society. I thought of the bright suns of passion and principle and where they lead us. To conviction, to commitment, occasionally to joy and, as often, to sacrifice. I thought of Hugo, of Norman Carr, of the scouts on patrol in the bush, of Chief Nsefu, of my grandfather. I thought of the red-brick World War I monument at Thiepal, France – 73 367 missing – small, neat figures in brass. I thought of the freedom that I, and a baby rhinoceros, had to walk across the fields where men had given their lives, committed their belief, to keep it that way.

# A WOUNDED BUFFALO

*As told by Joseph Kampamba*

It was on the 29th October last of last year. We were on patrol one day in the North Luangwa National Park, when on our journey we came across the footprints of poachers. We were suspecting that there were four poachers. We followed their footprints for many hours and found that the poachers had killed a common duiker on their way.

Later on the same day, while continuing following the footprints of the poachers, we came to a stream where we would like to drink some water. We found the poachers had also stopped to drink. Myself and my friend were walking on the other side of the stream and I stopped to drink some water. We noticed some blood next to the stream. Then I heard a voice say 'wooo'.

My friend had seen a wounded buffalo. There was no time. The buffalo charged me, he came for me. I grabbed for my firearm. My friend failed to shoot the buffalo and myself I tried to shoot but my firearm was not working, I suspect that the bullet was not good. The buffalo was still coming, he wanted to fight, but I am used to running. While I was running I tried to shoot the buffalo to scare him. My friend was putting another bullet in his gun. It was very bad.

The buffalo followed me, he came for my right. I threw my firearm on the ground and I jumped very high to try to catch a branch of a tree.

That buffalo came close to me but he missed me. Unfortunately the branch of the tree broke and I fell down into the stream and my toe got broken. My friend was going up the tree and shouting to make a lot of noise to chase the buffalo. The buffalo turned and came back again and, catching me in the stream, it hit me full on the chest. I failed to stand up. It was very, very, very bad. When he came close to my face I tried to catch on his horns and fight him. I held on to one horn with one arm but he saw the other arm stuck under that branch and he broke his horn into that arm. You can see the wounds here. He hit me on my side again in the same way. Then at last my friend who was on top of the tree managed to steady his firearm and shot that wounded buffalo.

He shot the buffalo in the backbone and it fell on top of me. It was very heavy and I was stuck. After some time my friend managed to squeeze me out from under the buffalo. He tore his shirt to stop my blood but my power was failing as we walked back to camp. It was nine kilometres away and we walked for two hours through the bush. I fell down many times.

From camp I was taken to Chungu Hospital. I think that is the power of God to survive in that way.

**ABOVE** *Game scout Joseph Kampamba (right) tells his story to scout Julius Chinkumba, who translates.*

**OPPOSITE, ABOVE** *Timothy Khozah. Well-armed scouts on random patrols have dramatically reduced poaching in North Luangwa.*

**ABOVE**  *Issuing clear and cool from the heights of the Muchinga Escarpment, the Mwaleshi River encounters a series of small falls before entering the flat land of the Luangwa Valley floor. North Luangwa.*

**LEFT**  *Leopard. North Luangwa.*

**OPPOSITE, ABOVE**  *Hugo van der Westhuizen begins a dawn patrol in his doorless aircraft. North Luangwa.*

**OPPOSITE, BELOW**  *A buffalo crosses the Lubanga River. North Luangwa.*

**PAGE 176, ABOVE**  *Barbel, a major source of crocodile food, squeal and grunt when they are caught;* **BELOW** *Turning leaf. Miombo woodland, North Luangwa.*

**PAGES 178/179**  *Pelicans, storks and egrets gather at the bounty of a drying lagoon. Nsefu Sector, South Luangwa.*

# ADRENALIN GRASS

I hear the soft footfall of Lloyd Mwale, the camp attendant, and the metallic clink of the enamel jug on its basin as he brings hot water to our grass-and-reed hut. He clears his throat and utters a discreet, 'Morning.' Peter answers, always wide awake at dawn and quietly preparing himself for the day ahead.

The moon has long set and it is still dark, and it is with difficulty that I overcome the strong desire to turn over under the blankets and return to my dream, to lie half-awake listening to the sound of the Verreaux's eagle-owl calling to its mate, the waking sound of the Luangwa Valley. My mind is made up for me as the powerful reverberation of a male lion's roar echoes up from the dry riverbed, right below our deck. This is answered by another, more distant roar. There is something urgent afoot, the two lions roar and grunt their challenge across the plain without pause for perhaps five minutes. A hyaena cackles between the roaring, as if unable to control itself in the potent tension.

Soon there is the suggestion of light in the sky, the stars fade and the shapes of tall trees emerge from the darkness. I catch a glimpse of Peter's broad grin as he passes my bed, cameras in hand, on his way to the campfire for coffee.

The lion roars again, closer, if that is possible. I feel like the hyaena sounds, nervous and eager as I dress quickly, tripping over things in my hurry to cover my nakedness with warm clothing. The camp is stirring to life now as there is sound everywhere, and the tropical boubou sings a lyrical background to the chitter and bustle of the birds coming awake. A breeze stirs the groundcover of leaves fallen from the trees, and dust swirls around my boots as I splash my face with water at the open-air basin. I arrive at the campfire to hear Stephen Banda, our guide, speaking of the leopard he had heard just before he blew out the camp lanterns and went to bed.

I remember now that I too had heard the sound. I had shaken Peter awake to listen. It was so close, perhaps we could see the leopard in the moonlight? The puku, normally calm in the proximity of the camp, had whistled their shrill alarm and run. We could dimly make out their ghostly shapes chasing back and forth on the open plain which lay across the river bed from the camp. Then we heard the growling, snarling sound of a struggle – intense and muted all at once – then everything had gone still, as if the night itself was startled into silence.

We are telling Stephen about what we had heard when the puku and impala on the open plain begin alarm-calling, whistling and snorting. They stand riveted, heads erect, eyes transfixed by what is passing through the long grass that runs to the right of the plain. Stephen and Peter are scanning the spiny amber-coloured grass with binoculars for a sign of what is there.

Lloyd arrives with freshly brewed coffee and our three companions on the walking safari join us at the fire. Stephen makes up his mind to find out what is unfolding here and suggests we leave our breakfast and come with him. 'In 10 minutes it may be too late,' he says as we grab cameras and binoculars and try to keep up with him.

Christopher Sakala, the armed scout allocated to our safari, materialises unannounced in front of Stephen and we quickly leave the security of the camp, cross the Chikoko riverbed and walk out onto the dew-laden plain. There are no vehicles here, no tracks. We are in the Remote Africa Safaris' guided walking safari bushcamp.

Christopher, tall with clean-cut features and engaging brown eyes, and Stephen, his charming smile gone to seriousness, are locked in an earnest, soft-toned exchange. Stephen throws some sand into the air to check the direction of the wind and we turn to walk downwind from the alarmed puku and impala.

Christopher points to some elephants emerging from the long grass to the far left of the plain. It is a breeding herd of seven, but we are downwind of them and they remain feeding on grass roots. Something is changing in me, I can feel it. I become aware of the wind on my face and am listening intently, reading the tracks we are walking over. I do not move on until I am certain. I do not look at the bush but into it as if my life depended on it, I steel myself and look back at the elephants. Peter and I usually conduct our photographic excursions from our Land Rover and I am unused to being on foot, among wild animals with no vehicle for support. I feel strangely unfamiliar, yet alive, as if even the air itself were a live thing. I am more secure with the sound of Peter's footfall behind me and the understated, quiet confidence of Stephen

**ABOVE**  *Sundowners. Remote Africa Safaris, Tafika Camp.*

**OPPOSITE, ABOVE**  *The Luangwa River makes its serpentine course through the flat country of its broad valley.*

**OPPOSITE, BELOW**  *Chamilandu Camp has a view across the river of the Chindeni Hills. South Luangwa.*

and Christopher, yet in my heart I know, if the situation becomes dangerous, I will have to draw on my own wits and courage and perhaps even speed and agility.

I smile to myself to find, when I lift my camera to photograph a group of puku etched by sunlight against the shiny darker grass, that I am shaking slightly. Looking through the lens relaxes me as I scan the distance for an image to capture this single moment.

Light floods the land now, bringing a shiny, glistening dawn. The chill of the June night has left a fine dew on the grass stalks and the air is crisp but a little smoky from a distant bushfire. I notice a faint jasmine fragrance mixed in with it and am listening to the different bird calls, when a puku whistle stuns me, not 20 metres away.

Christopher and Stephen turn and, with terse hand signals, direct us to follow them more closely and stay absolutely quiet as we pass through a patch of long grass to reach the plain on the other side. I turn to Peter and he is looking unsettled; he is extremely wary of walking though long grass where there is no view of what lies behind or within it. He asks Stephen if there is no other way.

The puku start to run around the far side of us, but still with all 30 or so heads staring exactly in the direction in which we are heading.

We take to the long grass and hurriedly, but as silently as possible, emerge on the far side.

Adrenalin is bitter on my tongue and I take a deep breath as I exchange glances with Christopher, hoping to communicate that I am uncomfortable and right behind him. He grins confidently, then returns his concentration to the task of keeping us safe as we stalk the unseen predator. We walk on, one step at a time. Suddenly the life on the plain erupts and puku and impala race in a blur to higher ground, further away from us. A fish-eagle calls and takes to the air and, directly in our path, two lions stand in the grass thicket.

The world stands still. Sound fades away. The fresh dawn smell is exquisite as it squeezes through my chest. In slow motion, or so it seems to me, a towering black-maned lion and his lithesome tawny mate stand to look at us, then ever so slowly they turn away and disappear back into the grass.

We stare in the direction of where the lions lay. Christopher has instructed us to stand our ground. It is long minutes before we relax and are once again a scout, a guide and five people from faraway lands on a foot-safari in Zambia.

Perhaps I imagined it, but there seemed to be a new bond between our small group as we return to camp and settle hungrily to our fine

breakfast of papaya, fresh-baked muffins, breads and slices of boiled egg and bacon, and make our second attempt at hot, steamy coffee. At first our conversation is sparse, but as the puku and impala begin to graze again out on the plain in front of the camp we too relax enough to touch tentatively on our shared experience.

I joke with Stephen about our safari beginning on such a high note, and ask how he is going to keep us amused for five days. He answers with a wry smile and tells me, 'in the wild nothing is certain'.

Yesterday, while walking into camp after being paddled across the Luangwa River, we had crossed the tracks of perhaps a thousand buffalo heading in the direction of the river. Stephen suggests now that we might find them and so, at 07h30, when most people's days are just beginning, we again fall in behind Christopher and Stephen.

We skirt the tree-lined Chikoko River for some time as, at each of the stagnant pools still remaining from the rainy season, there is life to see, and the warming day has stirred the forest creatures into activity. The first pool is the size of a small lagoon and about 60 baboons are silhouetted and bathed by the sun. There are many babies in this group and we watch enamoured by the adults' playfulness and affection and tolerant patience towards the babies. Every so often a bloodcurdling, high-pitched shriek sounds out as a small group of youngsters hurtles above our heads in mock terror, chastised by the dominant male.

Peter finds leopard tracks and we wonder if our camp leopard from the night had moved this way. We presume it is no longer here as the baboons are feeding calmly.

Cautiously a group of plump waterbuck with their white-encircled rumps comes to drink and, behind the treeline, with exhaustive caution, Thornicroft's giraffe linger and watch us. I look and listen. The forest along the river is saturated with sound and it is only when I step on a large stick that the snapping announces my passing. We come to another pool filling a deep gully off to the side of the river, with a fallen tree in its midst. Next to the tree a hippopotamus with a deeply lacerated hide lies bleeding and asleep. The injuries are almost certainly from a fight and I

am horrified by the apparent violence that has driven this hapless beast so far from the Luangwa River, where he must have become a threat to the dominant male.

Our coming upon this hippopotamus is too sudden to plan our correct upwind approach. Our scent startles him ruthlessly into wakefulness. He rises painfully and trundles out of the haven of the riverbed to a future too uncertain to contemplate.

I notice the etched tracks of hyaena passing next to the pool and shiver involuntarily as I see, too, drops of the hippopotamus' blood in the wet sand next to the tracks. I struggle to keep from my mind the images and sounds of the hippopotamus fights I have witnessed in the past, and it is with relief that dust and the low moan of buffalo on the move distract my dark thoughts. Stephen and Christopher have stopped walking and are engaged in the

low tones of Biza, their native Zambian language. I look in the direction in which they are pointing, to the other side of the Chikoko River where, as a breeze parts the dust, 600 or so buffalo move like black water between the trees. The dark-horned mass is both frightening and spectacular. It is widely believed that buffalo in a herd are not as much of a threat as the solitary old bachelor bulls known as 'dagga boys', which are notoriously bad tempered and aggressive. Buffalo in a herd tend to desire its cohesiveness and are inclined to rather flee from danger, the foreign and the unknown.

Our scent will carry on the wind and Stephen is convinced this will turn them away from us, back into the secrecy of the forest. We watch, acutely aware of their size, as they lift their heads and hold their horns high in response to our strange scent. Then slowly, some heavy with reticence, they move away. I hear others, alarmed by the unseen danger, crash senselessly through the trees.

Peter notices a smaller breakaway herd across the river from us emerging from thick impenetrable bush. They are unaware of our presence, moving towards us, perhaps to join the larger body of the herd. We are downwind of these buffalo so they will only see us when they are almost upon us or if we move. This may bring them yet closer still as, without our scent to appease their curiosity, they will need to approach us.

For the first time the tension in Christopher and Stephen is apparent. Our group is trapped next to a deep fissure in a dry part of the Chikoko riverbed, between two arms of a divided buffalo herd. Christopher leads us down into the riverbed, a perfect escape route, as the sides appear too steep for buffalo at this point. He walks far ahead to check for unseen danger before Stephen guides us forward.

My mouth is dry and I am aware of the tense, drawn faces around me. From the base of the riverbed we cannot see the source of our

danger, only sense and imagine it. As the smell of buffalo, rank and dusty, permeates the air, I confuse it with the smell of fear.

Christopher backtracks to us and tells Stephen he has found a way out of the riverbed, ahead of the buffalo. Peter and I exchange long looks; we are both searching for a tall, sturdy, easy-to-climb tree. Once we have passed one, we look ahead for another. Then, rifle at the ready, Christopher leads us up the steep bank and into the forest again. There are fresh buffalo signs everywhere, but the dust is swirling behind us as the buffalo find a crossing and rejoin the splinter herd, where we had stood only a few minutes before.

Stephen is looking ahead of us through his binoculars. An old wily male buffalo with a huge spread of mud-encrusted horns, which gleam in the mid-morning sun, is roused from sleep and charges out of the riverbed. He is soon joined by two more 'dagga boys', which had been resting in the shade of a spreading old marula tree.

The buffalo turn, heads high, and bleary, blood-flecked eyes bore down at our small group. We stare back and try as best as possible to mask the fear which must be naked in our eyes. Instinctive enemies, we wait, hearts racing, legs turned to jelly, for their next move. We stand like this for a lifetime. I see, hear and smell the wild world with ferocious intensity, my breath tight in my body.

Christopher from behind stands rigid, the muscles in the side of his face taut, his gun cocked. Seconds seem like hours, then, unbearably slowly and even gracefully, the buffalo turn and with heads down and enormous hindquarters following, they leave us alone.

Stephen decides it is rest time. Time for tea, a pause to gather ourselves. He leads us to a tranquil, shaded lagoon covered almost completely by the luminescent green of a blanket of water weed. The

normality of a cup of tea brewed on a bush fire by Moffat Gondwe, the porter of our party, and the soft, delectable taste of home-baked cookies is the comfort I long for and I sit quietly and toss small seed pods into the water, taking pleasure in the way they float away. Stephen has chosen a place with thick shade and a clear view to approaching animals, except to the one side of us where the forest grows almost up to the edge of the lagoon. Two of our company lie down flat, with eyes closed, on the cool earth and I listen to the crackling of Moffat's small kettle fire.

Moffat lays out a bright tablecloth and serves our tea. Baboons pick between the fallen seed pods and grass shoots, butterfly wings flash orange over the water and I look for owls in the deep camouflage of the thick green foliage of the mature trees. A shadow passes across the sun and the lagoon's shine is dulled. I turn to where the forest meets the lagoon and there, in a gap in the trees, like ghosts, without a sound, a breeding herd of elephants has come to drink.

In lightning seconds Christopher is among us, whispering 'Do not run'. And again, 'Do not run', this time more softly but with greater intent. Our scent is carried directly away from the unsuspecting elephants. They continue out of the forest, perhaps 15 metres away, and line the sandy banks of the shallow lagoon opposite our tea party. The baboons continue their earnest feeding without interruption and two Egyptian geese float out of hiding, away from the elephants, into open water. One after the other, the elephants stretch their trunks far out and tentatively pry the waterweed apart to reach the water. The older elephants are adept at this and drink first. The smallest calf, days old, screams in high-pitched frustration at not being able to reach the water.

It is the first sound from these elephants. The matriarch reacts sharply and rushes to the baby's side. I think she senses our presence, but we are downwind of her and crouching dead still. She shakes her head and ears and lifts her trunk into the wind. She puts her trunk back into the water to bring water to her baby, but does not complete the action, she is uncomfortable. Silently, swiftly, she turns from the lagoon and, in one body, the herd follows her back into the haven of the forest on the far side and they are gone. I accept Moffat's proffered cup of hot, smoke-flavoured tea and, clasping its warmth to my hands, I sit and wait for them to return.

**ABOVE** *The quiet wading of an elephant leaves a clear watermark on its legs, showing the depth of its chosen crossing point.*

**OPPOSITE** *A herd of puku.*

**TOP** *Game scout Christopher Sakala and a lone buffalo warily watch each other. Chikoko Trails walking safari, South Luangwa.*

**ABOVE** *Game scout Isaiah Nyirenda watches over Phil Berry, one of the present-day pioneers of the Luangwa Valley, and Babette Alfieri, who arrived in Africa as an adult with a small suitcase, two full sets of Land Rover tyres, 144 pairs of socks, several crates of motor spares and other sundry articles.*

**OPPOSITE** *Impala. South Luangwa.*

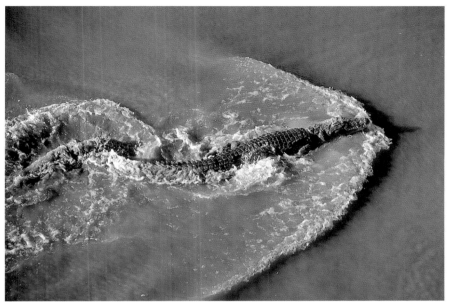

*I have at times been fortunate to be in country with another who is familiar with it. Someone who knows its details, perceives its mood and is sensitive to the shift in its nuance. It is rewarding and, like walking with your shirt off, seems to bring you closer to that which surrounds you. Flying the Luangwa Valley with John Coppinger was like that. Like being, for a while, included in the easy company of two old friends.*

**ABOVE**  *A crocodile surges from the bank.*

**LEFT**  *A pod of hippopotamus scatters as two bulls fight.*

**ABOVE**  *A hippopotamus carcass is a banquet for crocodiles and, in the Luangwa River, can draw gatherings of a hundred or more leviathans together. A live hippopotamus, however, is a fearless adversary of the crocodile.*

**OPPOSITE**  *As we flew, drove and walked beside the turning landscapes of the Luangwa River, photographing its extraordinary gatherings of hippopotamus and crocodile, a song kept surfacing in my head: Keb Mo's 'I love muddy water, it's dirty but it feels all right'. Luangwa River, North Luangwa.*

**TOP**  *Puku feeding in a dry lagoon. Nsefu Sector, South Luangwa.*

**ABOVE, LEFT TO RIGHT**  *Chikoko Trails Camp. Leopard. Chamilandu Camp dining area.*

**OPPOSITE**  *Puku stand on the cracked surface of a dry lagoon, beside what was a hippopotamus path. South Luangwa.*

*There are places in the Luangwa Valley today where one can encounter the Africa that, a century and a half ago, drew the young and brave from their comfort and conformity in Europe, and inspired Joseph Conrad to put pen to paper.*

# TANZANIA

## NGORONGORO & THE SERENGETI

# Ngorongoro Conservation Area

I have always felt sadness for those rhinoceros and lion I have seen in the zoos of Europe, standing there in the snow and drab, grey cold. It seemed a far, harsh reach from the country of our home. I was surprised therefore on my first visit to the Ngorongoro Conservation Area to find that, at three degrees south of the equator, it was not the hot Africa that one might expect at these latitudes. This was not Conrad's Africa of steamy jungle and torpid rivers. It was more a hobbit land, a country of cool gladed forests, of secret valleys, still waterless plains, old volcanoes and Mordorian peaks.

The reason is that the 8 292 square kilometres of the Ngorongoro Conservation Area encompass a high-altitude plateau of between 1 500 and 3 600 metres above sea level. The Ngorongoro Crater stands on the very southern edge of this plateau, with its south-eastern side falling precipitously from the heights of the crater rim through a sheer escarpment to the Great Rift Valley far below. The Ngorongoro Crater is in fact the peak of a mountain and, during the dry winter months from June to October, temperatures may fall below freezing. Even in midsummer, on the heights of the crater, the evenings are cool and the nights chilly.

The virtually permanently cold nights of the heights, however, render them naturally malaria free and veteran African explorer Frederick Courtney Selous recommended them as a respite from heat and repetitive bouts of malaria.

**ABOVE, LEFT**  *The typical stance of the Maasai moran.*

**BELOW**  *Dr Peter Morkel, Africa's veterinary expert on black rhinoceros, checks the Frankfurt Zoological Society aeroplane that sports the distinctive zebra-stripe design initiated by its founder, Dr Bernard Grzimek of* Serengeti Shall Not Die *fame.*

Rain falls mostly during summer throughout the whole of the Ngorongoro Conservation Area, but during January and February one can expect periods of dry weather. The rain itself, however, is seldom of a nature to spoil a safari as it falls in short showers or brief extravagant storms. It is during this summer season that clouds often gather about the peaks, causing them to be fog-bound. Rains render the hard-packed, red-earth roads as slippery as an ice rink, making passage on the narrow roads of the rim and the winding descent of the escarpment a mud-spattered, mist-shrouded, cautious affair.

The thin-veined streams and springs, trickling and dripping from the cool heights of the forests that are trapped within the crater itself, gather in three lakes in depressions of the valley floor. Lake Magadi and Gorigor Swamp expand and recede dramatically with the seasons but there is, none the less, permanent water within the crater. There is therefore no seasonal fluctuation in game viewing potential, except perhaps that in summer the crater floor supports a tall savanna of verdant grass in which a recumbent animal is more difficult to see.

Outside of the isolated realm of Ngorongoro's great caldera, on the western plains of the Ngorongoro Conservation Area, the seasons have a more obvious cycle. In winter, a fine veil of dust lifts from the dry earth and, combined with the smoke of frequent wild fires, it casts an opaque shroud over the far reach of the land, often spoiling the light for those with serious photographic intentions. The summer rains cleanse the air and bring a flush of fresh green life to these short grass plains. In response, between December and May, the vast herds of wildebeest and zebra end their southerly migration here, dropping their calves to coincide with the brief abundance of the wet season's plenty.

The Ngorongoro Conservation Area is, moreover, a central area to Maasai pastoralists. It is here, in these rolling green hills and on the shimmering dry plains, that one may encounter that champion of my youth, stumble on that quintessential African scene – the lone, red-robed man walking with his ornately branded herds between groups of zebra and giraffe, standing with his long-bladed spear between a surly lion and his wealth. Most Maasai here, despite a sometimes fierce appearance, are tolerant of visitors and accept without animosity curiosity about their singular lives. They will generally overlook any minor cultural *faux pas* that we may make in our unenlightened enquiry, but it should be remembered that respect of their livestock is paramount and to enter a kraal ahead of a Maasai family member is a blatant affront, and doubly so if perpetrated by a woman.

The Maasai were, however, not the first to inhabit this area and, on the bone-jarring transit from Ngorongoro to the Serengeti, it is well worth the respite from the manic, pounding madness of the road to turn off to visit the Olduvai Gorge archaeological diggings, where 3.5-million-year-old fossils reveal that the root of all mankind began in Africa.

ABOVE   *Maika Olkerii, a soft-smiled local Maasai who guards the crater's rhinoceros population.*

PAGE 196   *The giant fever trees of the Lerai Forest dwarf an elephant bull.*

PAGES 198/9   *The Gorigor Swamp stands etched in silver reflection beneath a mantle of low cloud gathered within the crater.*

PAGES 202/203   *Succumbing to the opulent fantasy of the dining hall at Crater Lodge, Stella Kimei dances.*

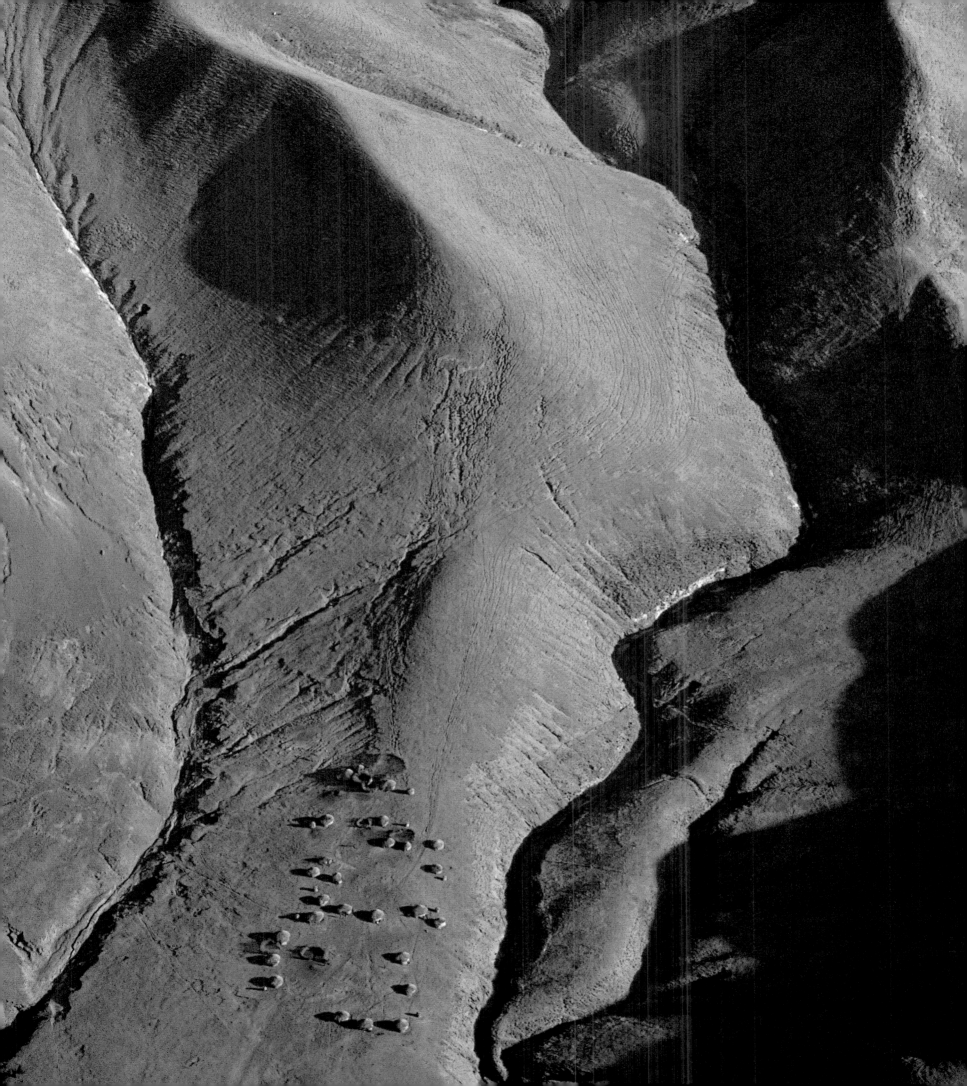

**PAGE 206**  *Still standing on the rim of extinction, Tanzania's black rhinoceros population has been slow to recover, despite effective protection.*

**PAGE 207**  *A lion and lioness beneath typically dramatic crater clouds.*

**PAGES 208/209**  *At the very depth of Ngorongoro's crater, flamingos feed in the shallows of Lake Magadi.*

**PREVIOUS SPREAD**  *In the maze-like valleys of the Empakaai foothills, Maasai live as traditionally as ever, their manyattas accessible only by way of arduous footpaths.*

**THIS SPREAD**  *A paradox of Ngorongoro is that, within the crater, the sheer rise of the rim dwarfs its beasts, but the drama of the setting has a reciprocal effect that adds weight to their presence.*

# WHERE GOD STEPPED DOWN

In Africa, there is a small bright star that hangs beside the sliver of the new moon as it sets. As the yellow cast of the sunset gives way to the purple onset of the night that settles so quickly in the tropics, they appear almost side by side above the western horizon. The thin and the bright – they are an incongruous but bewitchingly compatible couple, lingering only briefly on the stage before being swallowed by the dark presence of the land. With their going, the courtiers of the night are set free.

The hyaena are first, that distinctive whoop, so bold an utterance, a single-line hymn to 'wild'. It may perhaps seem strange that the hyaena are here at all, for this is neither a game reserve nor a park. The Ngorongoro Conservation Area is a declared World Heritage Site, but even its most famous component, the Ngorongoro Crater, with one of the densest concentrations of wildlife in the whole of Africa, is not a game reserve. From within the thorn-branch enclosure of the Maasai manyatta, outside of which the hyaena stalks, the Ngorongoro Crater is only faintly discernible on the profile of the far southern horizon by the cluster of clouds that gathers to tumble over its rim.

The hyaena calls again, closer than before, and the goats packed tightly within their own enclosure inside the manyatta can be heard shuffling in the darkness. The sweet tang of their fresh dung brings a farmyard familiarity to the night. A light breeze whispers through the thorns of the enclosure, carrying with it the fragrance of the dry savanna beyond and a sound not quite heard from the night on the other side. Sitting still to listen, there is nothing but the sound of a Maasai child asking something in a soft intimacy from within one of the three low, dome-shaped huts in the manyatta. It receives a curt answer and then all is still again except for the occasional sighing of the breeze. Even the hyaena has gone quiet.

There is no light issuing from any of the huts, for the Maasai, like most of Africa's rural people beyond the reach of electricity, have turned in not long after darkness settled. They will rise, long before we are accustomed, at the first promise of light in the eastern sky. Between the huts the embers of the fire glow like dull red eyes in the black face of the night but offer no light.

This is these sleeping people's permanent home and the Ngorongoro Conservation Area is Maasai land. The Maasai tribe are spread between central Kenya and central Tanzania, but it is the area on either side of the Kenya–Tanzania border that is their heartland. They are a fiercely traditional people and it is to their inimitable and singular cultural perceptions that much of East Africa's most important wilderness owes its existence. Hunting for meat is traditionally frowned upon in Maasai culture, for only a poor or hungry man hunts, and this reflects a failure in his managing and tending his herds. Cattle are more precious than gold to traditional Maasai.

For the more than 2 500 Maasai who live within the Ngorongoro Conservation Area it is more than just a heartland for it contains some of their most important spiritual places. Strangely, however, the most sacred of places to the Maasai, 'the place where God stepped down onto earth', the mountain of Ol Doinyo Lengai, lies just outside the north-eastern border of the Ngorongoro Conservation Area. At 2 878 metres, Ol Doinyo Lengai is still an active volcano, spewing a fetid breath of mud and steam into the tepid air of the tropics.

It is the last in a line of now-extinct volcanoes that stretches away to the south, leaving only passive, nutrient-rich craters as a reminder of their heyday. Empakaai, with its beautiful forest-fringed lake, Olmati and, most famous of them all, Ngorongoro.

Dawn on the rim of the Ngorongoro Crater is a close, opaque world suffused with gold as clouds settle on the rim and the world becomes a passage of swirling mists. The moisture the mists have to offer is frugal, but it is gathered drop by drop, drip by drip, by a dense green forest that crowds the southern crater rim and walls. Softly, the moisture falls to the ground and feeds a secret world beyond the sunlight where timid footfalls follow secret paths and the earth smells of dawn.

The mists play a game of hide-and-seek with reality, revealing sporadic moments of delight before jealously concealing them again; a giant spider web hung with dew delivers a jewel-like radiance in the momentary presence of the sun; an elephant, huge and still, swathed in a garland of green, standing silent in a muted world where the translucent curtain closes too soon on the wonders of its stage. Moving around the rim, the cloud draws back to reveal a glimpse of a land far below, briefly it obscures it again before offering a window through which the glint of water and a stand of trees appear clear in the warmth of the early sun. Suddenly, close by, an apparition appears like none before, three Maasai youths stand beside the road with painted faces, wraith-like, as if some ancient ancestor of the land had come to give us pause. The road starts downwards.

To descend the steep rim of Ngorongoro from the height of the clouds is to step through the looking glass of an African wonderland. The broad crater floor appears as a stage where the cast is an almost

---

**PREVIOUS SPREAD** *Maasai youths perform the traditional 'singolio' dance.*

**OPPOSITE** *Maasai women of the Ngorongoro highlands wear cloth we saw nowhere else.*

fantasy-like parade of Africa's wild denizens, a concentration of beasts almost without peer. All of the most beloved are here – the bloody and the stately, the stoic and the swift, the ugly and the cute. There are forests of towering, yellow-barked acacias where the tusks of other giants have gouged the history of their passing, and there are savannas wide enough for a herd of wildebeest to walk away until the sight of them becomes a possession of the imagination, eclipsed by the dancing waves of heat. And all of this is bound by the dramatic backdrop of the sheer sides of the walls.

Flocks of rose-pink flamingos chatter and squabble in the shallows of the lakes and move as one body in response to hyaenas that patrol the muddy shore searching for signs of the weak. A long-horned rhinoceros and her calf rest on their sides in a patch of cracked clay, their short-snorted breath raising rhythmic puffs of dust from the earth. Two cheetah stalk a gazelle from the cover of a gully, whilst high overhead vultures ride a thermal and watch and wait.

It is a world of the watching and the watched, the content and the hungry, the restful and the wary, the great, the quick and the dead. The tension only eases as one climbs the crater walls again to the sanctuary of the rim and the soft influences of the clouds.

In a lodge of truly eccentric design there is a grand bath where a bubble bath, scattered with rose petals and lit by a bank of candles, eases away the heat and hard roads of the day, while crystal glasses of champagne tease recollections with their effervescence.

It seems a distant world to this Maasai manyatta, where the senses have become so instinctively tuned. The breeze has strengthened and grown colder. The enclosure that encircles us is made from layered branches of whistling thorn, sharp, hostile, impenetrable. The base of the thorns are bulbous and, bored through by beetles, they whistle in the wind. They issue now a soft, eerie fluted note in the rising wind whose chill breath seems to be fanning the stars to an icy brightness. The cattle have become restless; the hyaena, silent, must be patrolling close by in the dark.

A spear glints in the meagre light. The Maasai man is here, his cloaked body vague in the dark. He peers for a long while into the night. Nothing can be seen until a shadow moves, softly outlined against the pale grass. It moves closer, pauses, and then comes closer still. Some stones and a stick thud against the ground out there and in an instant the shadow is gone and there is only the sound of something running steadily away into the rolling plain beyond.

**THIS SPREAD** *Once a month, the Maasai of Ngorongoro and the Eyasi escarpment don their finery and make their way to the local market, meeting to trade cattle and goods and share news.*

**FOLLOWING SPREAD, LEFT** *Burchell's zebra graze in a brief wash of sunlight that pierced the turmoil of cloud on the crater rim;*
**RIGHT** *Crater Lodge's celebrated after-game-drive rose-petal bath.*

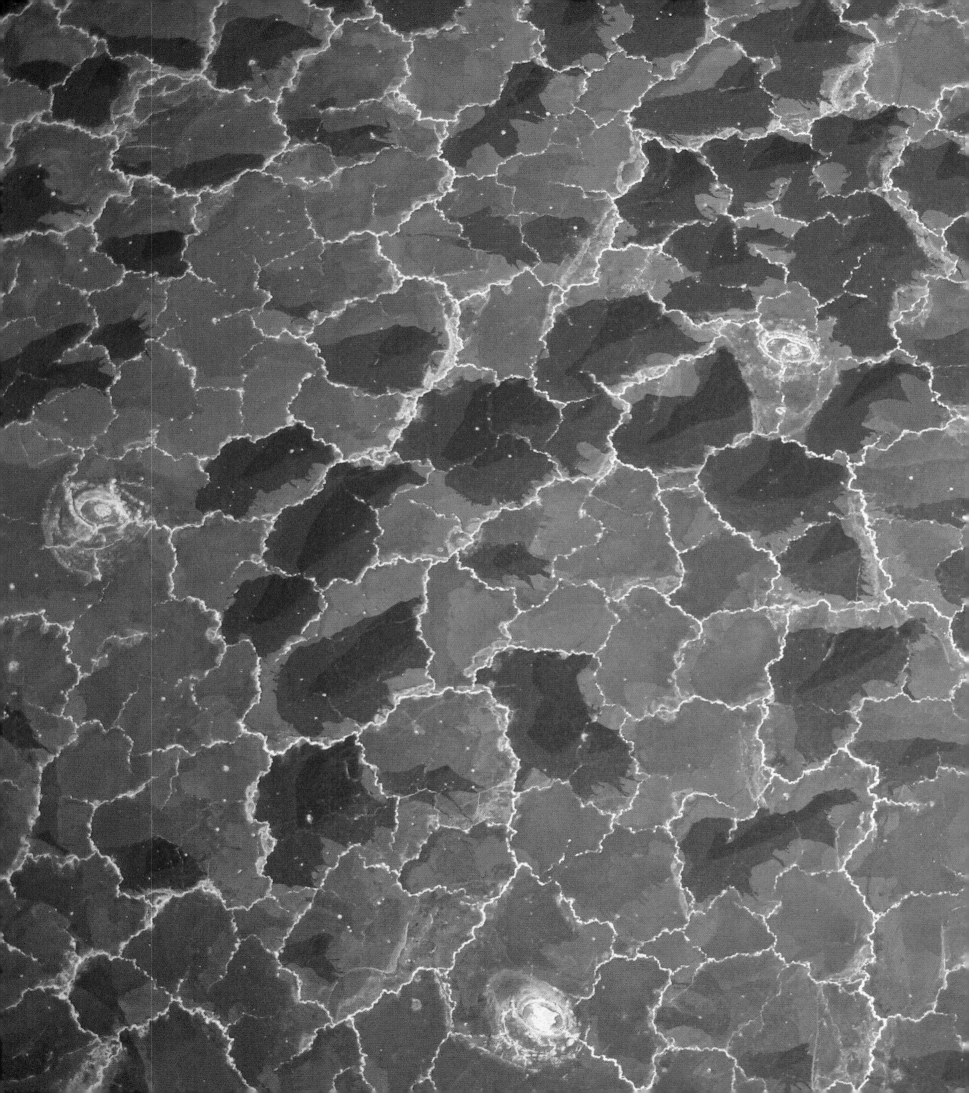

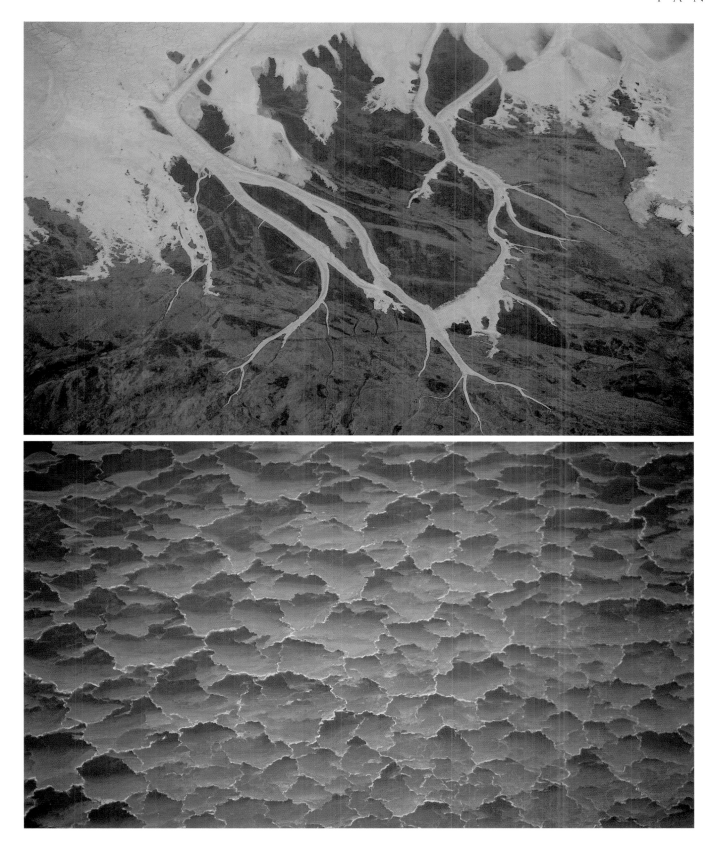

**TOP**  *Different-coloured silts leave the patterns of their receding on the Lake Eyasi shore.*

**ABOVE & OPPOSITE**  *As the nutrient-rich Lake Natron dries, minerals condense into vivid colours and myriad forms on its surface.*

**FOLLOWING SPREAD**  *The Maasai sacred mountain Ol Doinyo Lengai, the Mountain of God.*

# SERENGETI

A million years is an intangible sort of time, just a figure, not something to relate to. A hundred thousand years is not much better, still too big to grasp. At fifty thousand years I might be able to look out of the window at the land and see the valley formed by a river in a country of rolling hills or a great cliff or rock with a weathered face, but it remains elusive, difficult to comprehend the dramatic scope of time. At a thousand years, I think of Allah or Christ, of written history, but it is truly only a hundred years that lies clearly within my grasp.

In the year that I was born, the Serengeti National Park was only six years old. It seems so young. Why did we wait so long? The Serengeti did not just suddenly appear in time – it has been there forever, evolving, eroding, changing – but that it took so long to be recognised as one of the greatest natural spectacles on earth, virtually within my lifespan, seems only just in time.

It made me pause and consider. Perhaps not all evolution occurs in geological time. We do not know precisely how long the great migration of the Serengeti has been going on. Thousands of years at least, pre-biblical time. Perhaps it took that long just to begin – evolving slowly, shifting to the imperceptible cycle of change, gaining momentum.

The migration has no beginning or end. It is a circular motion, a cycle, driven by the seasons, reliant on the rain and therefore fickle, predictable only in the vaguest terms. It is at its stillest early in the new year, in January and February, when in response to the new grass the wildebeest are dropping their calves. At this point the animals have arrived at the southernmost turn of their march, many of them having moved beyond the borders of the Serengeti into the northern plains of the Ngorongoro Conservation Area.

Perhaps it was here that three thousand years ago the rock-art painters of Kondoa encountered them and rendered them on the sandstone walls of the Masai Escarpment in their complex overlaid paintings. But perhaps this is just fancy, as not even the Maasai had arrived this far south yet, let alone the caravan route from the coast that sought slaves and ivory in the interior, carrying them back to the ports of Bagamoyo, Zanzibar and Kilwa Kisiwani. Perhaps the animals were as plentiful that far south of the Serengeti then as they are in the protected arena of the Serengeti today.

Within six weeks of calving, the fragile, stick-legged calves of the wildebeest and foals of the zebra have grown and 1 300 000 wildebeest, 250 000 zebra, and scattered groups of Thomson's gazelle, eland and topi are on the move. Turning north and west, they pass through Seronera in the centre of the park. It was at this time, while the predators of Seronera feasted on the passing bounty, that Tanzania came into being in 1964.

In December 1963, Zanzibar had been granted independence. Within a month, however, the Arab-controlled government had been toppled and, in April 1964, Zanzibar became incorporated as part of Tanganyika and the new country of Tanzania was born, with one of Africa's true statesmen, Julius Nyerere, at the helm.

The march of the migration through history is inexorable. After Seronera, long columns, winding across the land like an infestation of giant snakes, walk with nodding heads towards the west, raising a fine dust. I recall in these black serpentine columns, the snake dances of the Sukuma who live to the south and west of the Serengeti. To a staccato drum beat, these dancers wind the thick coils of a live python around themselves. The drumming follows a 'Zorba the Greek' style, increasing in tempo until the frenetic gyrations of the dancer make the gigantic snake so agitated and excited that the audience often scatters. The dances mark the harvest celebrations and usually start in June when the migration begins to arrive in the Western Corridor.

The Western Corridor is a wide valley, rimmed both north and south by a country of fine hills that jut through the plain. It is a country favoured by the elephants and it would be interesting to know if elephants ever formed part of the migration. Today the elephants are few and although they move, they do not follow the body of the migration. In the past, the past still within the grasp of our rationale, there were more, far more elephants, enough to support the constant demand of a lucrative ivory trade.

In 1857 the explorer Richard Burton, visiting the towns of Tanga and Pangani on the coast of Tanzania, reported that 70 000 pounds of ivory passed through Tanga each year and wrote 'Pangani, I am told, exports annually 35 000 pounds of ivory, 1 750 pounds of black rhinoceros horn and 16 pounds of hippopotamus teeth.' The persecution of the elephant and rhino of Africa continues even today, despite an international

**ABOVE**  *Maasai moran tend their wealth.*

**OPPOSITE**  *The Serengeti wildebeest migration, one of earth's great natural phenomena.*

ban on trade in ivory and rhino horn. Less than 50 black rhinoceros are left in the combined area of the Serengeti and the Ngorongoro Conservation Area and the elephants of the Serengeti's Western Corridor are wary and ill tempered.

In the centre of the Western Corridor, the migrating animals must cross the natural barrier of the Grumeti River. It is an annual feast for the crocodiles of the Grumeti and we have watched riveted as crocodile after crocodile has slid past us in the still, stagnant pools of the river towards the calling of a herd of wildebeest approaching the water to cross.

country. Nyerere received no support, financial or otherwise, from the United Nations or any of the major powers and was even criticised by some African countries. He did it alone and almost crippled Tanzania.

The wildebeest, though, like history, move on and by November are usually back in the Serengeti, headed south towards the calving grounds. It was on 10 November 1871 that Henry Morton Stanley found David Livingstone at Ujiji, on the shores of Lake Tanganyika and uttered the famous 'Dr Livingstone, I presume?'

Eighty years later the Serengeti National Park was proclaimed. It is remarkable the change those 80 years wrought upon

Once through the trial of the Grumeti, the migration spreads out across a broad front and, as a rule, moves north and eastward, through the Lobo area and the Ikorongo controlled area, which is outside the park's boundaries. Towards the latter part of the year the animals start crossing the unfenced border into Kenya through the Masai Mara, the northernmost turn of the migration. By October the bulk of the migrating animals are in Kenya, and the Serengeti feels as lonely as Julius Nyerere must have felt in 1979 when he sent the Tanzanian army into Uganda and toppled Africa's most notorious dictator, Idi Amin. Amin's reign of terror had reached the proportions of a megalomaniacal madness, of genocide, where every intellectual was considered an enemy of the state and the possession of spectacles was sufficient to infer intellectual status. More than 300 000 people had died and many more fled the

the land. Eighty years of commerce and guns. The wildebeest move in a circle of time, driven by a compulsion far greater than any individual life. And yet this powerful instinct, that took who knows how long just to begin, has been eclipsed by the arrival of men from faraway lands. I am one of them and, sitting on the granite domes of the Moru Koppies beneath a hot African sun, watching the great black mass of the animals, thousands upon thousands of dots moving across the plains, leaves me wondering at what we have done.

**TOP** *The areas of black rhinoceros strongholds in the Serengeti have been placed off limits to tourism.*

**RIGHT** *Lion dummy used in research.*

**OPPOSITE** *A lioness stalks a topi over open ground.*

**ABOVE & OPPOSITE, BELOW** *The Serengeti Balloon Safari is one of the most iconic of its genre, a romantic recollection of Europe's exploration of Africa.*

*As a child, I pored over the black-and-white images of lion, Maasai and big-wheeled aircraft in Grzimek's book,* Serengeti Shall Not Die. *Later, in my youth, I did the same with the work of Elliot Porter and Hugo van Lawick, until finally I stood before it myself; moved, as were my predecessors, by so vast and unspoilt a tract of Africa.*

**THIS SPREAD & THE FOLLOWING** *The crocodiles were moving before we heard the wildebeest. Armour-plated giants coming fast, splashing across the shallows and then sinking away to rippleless silence in the deep drinking pools. The wildebeest and the zebra, nervous and fretful on the bank, coming closer, turning back. My palms sweaty on the camera. The sound of the herd on the air and my heart loud in my ears. Grumeti River, Serengeti Western Corridor.*

**PAGE 238, ABOVE** *Wildebeest. Western Corridor;*
**BELOW** *Lion. Ndutu.*

**PAGE 239, ABOVE** *Elephant and hot-air balloon. Seronera;*
**BELOW** *Burchell's zebra and white-bearded wildebeest take fright. Maasai Koppies.*

**PAGES 240/241** *Near Seronera.*

# KENYA

## Masai Mara, Amboseli & Tsavo

# MASAI MARA & LAKE NAKURU

I was singing on that road from Narok to the Masai Mara. That road. That road where the drop off at the edge of the tar is high enough for traffic-numb goats to seek shade in the lee of it, that road where the bus and truck drivers seem determined to put the quality of your nerves to the test. That road that transforms from smooth tar to a potholed nightmare in the space of a few metres and stays that way for longer, that road that ends abruptly in unfinished road works and, like the frayed end of a rope, spreads out across the country in a maze of tracks that billow choking clouds of dust. That signpostless road, that endless corrugation, that road, the main road to the Masai Mara.

'Who wants to be lonely? No not me, no not me,' I was singing to Dani Klein which, in retrospect, was quite apt. She is diminutive, almost tiny in stature with a voice that is so big and powerfully individual and a style that is engagingly unique that, seeing her live, one is spellbound, captivated. The Masai Mara is much the same.

At 1 500 square kilometres the Masai Mara is not a big reserve, diminutive in comparison to some of the others in Africa and yet, as a destination, it is one of the most sought after. Why? The migration? Yes, that. But it is more than that. The Maasai? That too, but the Masai Mara is more than the sum of its parts. Perhaps it is the 'white mischief' component that lends it its intangible, yet pronounced eccentricity. It is unexpected, unusual, attractive and compelling.

I have a veterinarian schoolfriend who is married to a Kenyan. He is eccentric enough to be Kenyan himself. Self-described as 'sticking his fingers into poodles' so that he can spend the money he makes keeping the same finger on Africa's wildlife pulse, he considers the Kenyan contingent of his family to be 'Penga! All bloody penga'.

Where else in the world do the cowboys wear skirts, go barefoot and have as pronounced an inclination to getting pissed, getting laid, or going for a long walk with a Maasai friend, and not necessarily in that order, as they do for creeping up to lions?

We saw lions before we saw the entrance gate. Well, glimpses of lions between the minibuses. The track we were on bypassed the inconvenience of the entrance gate, going straight into the unfenced reserve. We had to back track about two kilometres towards a radio mast that speared the sky. The fees we paid there went to the Narok District Council.

The Masai Mara is not a national park but a national reserve, falling under the jurisdiction of the Narok District Council for all the land east of the Mara River, and the Trans-Mara District Council for the triangle west of the river. The differentiation between a national park and a national reserve is described by the National Park Trustees as '... a local term denoting an area for preservation where

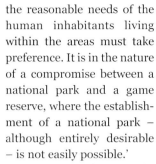

the reasonable needs of the human inhabitants living within the areas must take preference. It is in the nature of a compromise between a national park and a game reserve, where the establishment of a national park – although entirely desirable – is not easily possible.'

The Maasai live on the periphery of the reserve and their population is growing, whilst their strict adherence to the credo that hunting is beneath them is slipping. Dr Robin Reid and Michael Rainy conducted surveys of the greater Masai Mara area in 1999 and 2002 and reported that the number of Maasai homesteads had increased by 11 per cent. They established too that there was as much wildlife in pastoral grazing areas adjacent to the reserve as in the reserve itself. They found that the presence of people and livestock attracted wildlife to an area by creating short-grass areas around settlements, where nutrients are high and predators more scarce and conspicuous. The survey noted that less than one per cent of the Maasai land was farmed or fenced.

I remember watching a mixed herd of wildebeest and zebra divide to walk past a trading store on a hill in the Narok portion of the reserve. A pick-up with sagging springs was parked in front, on the store's bare, gully-eroded yard, held still by a rock behind the wheel. Several Maasai were waiting without urgency outside and a goat nibbled at some growth against the building. Neither the animals nor the people changed their pace or their attitude and the herd reformed to graze slowly on.

The eccentricity of the Masai Mara is accentuated by the fact that it is actually a reserve with two hats. The western triangle of the Mara, under the jurisdiction of the Trans-Mara Council and managed under contract by the Mara Conservancy, is more consistent with other African parks in its management. It has maintained and signposted roads, regular patrols, and the entrance road actually passes through Oloololo Gate, the main entrance to the western triangle. Across the river to the east, the Narok District Council area is self-managed and has a far more *laissez-faire* attitude, reminiscent of the Africa one finds away from the tourist path. Nowhere is the split persona of the Masai Mara more apparent than at the river crossings of the migration.

We had been parked on the edge of the Mara River since dawn, waiting for a group of about 700 wildebeest to cross. As the day warmed, their numbers had swelled. I could see the slowly plodding columns that drained them

them from the plains to this pause beside the river. By mid-morning there were perhaps twice as many and beside us the vehicles formed a line abreast. The first wildebeest were cautiously approaching the river about 250 metres away. A guide, tired of waiting, threaded his vehicle through the waiting cars and, despite shouts of derision, had driven between the milling herd and the water, spooking the wildebeest back away from the river. On their far side he had climbed down from his vehicle and walked to the edge to show his clients the crocodiles, which had all slid silently beneath the surface by the time they arrived. He then opted to have his picnic right there. I thought a skirt-clad cowboy a few cars away might take him out, but he just shook his head and took the opportunity of the delay to offer a round of 'G & T'.

It took some time for the animals to return to the river's edge after the guide had left, but by midday there were more than 2 000 waiting to cross. The vehicles now stood three deep. Across the river, on the western side, the only official vehicle I saw in our entire time in the Masai Mara had ordered the vehicles there well clear of the exit points from the river. They were parked neatly on the edge of the road, or on high ground, and everyone was within their cars.

The official then started flashing his lights at the cars stacked willy-nilly on our side, trying to get those people sitting on the roofs back into their vehicles. He was largely ignored. Right behind us a minibus trying to squeeze forward got stuck in the thick ooze of a mud puddle. There was a great deal of revving, but the minibus stayed put. A few drivers climbed down to have a look and stood smoking and shaking their heads as the wheels spun. From across the river the warden, standing on the seat of his Jeep, shouted something. The stuck driver bellowed back and there was a brief cross-river exchange before the driver climbed down and, dismissing the hapless warden with a wave, ignored him. And just then the wildebeest started to cross.

For 15 minutes or more, I saw nothing except what was in the lens. I was dimly aware of the cacophony, but my ears were tuned to Beverly's instructions as to where I should concentrate and to her hasty supply of film, as the shutters of our cameras clicked with a frenetic urgency. As the wildebeest moved forward to cross, they were drawn steadily downstream towards the cars. Eventually they were right below us, 15 metres away, when the lead animal looked up, paused and then, with eyes wide with fright, turned and ran. The whole herd followed. I took my eye

from the lens and only managed to half strangle the yell of outrage that burst from my chest.

A neat American family in Bermuda shorts and white socks were edging past the front of our vehicle, cameras poised, right above the wildebeest. They looked at me in shock. The wildebeest were gone. Behind me, more than 200 people lined the bank, others were running to join them. The driver was still spinning in the mud hole, alternately splattering those hurrying by with mud behind and in front of him as he changed between forward and reverse. A Japanese and an Italian man, both red in the face, were pushing at each other's chests right on the edge of the bank. A camera lay in the grass on the ground. People craned over the shoulders of those in front and a fat man shook himself like a wet dog to push them back and then composed a picture. A porcelain-skinned woman in a soft yellow straw-hat, standing in the roof hatch of a lime-green Land Rover, asked a question of the Maasai man on the roof of the car beside her. As he turned to answer, from my angle, the same angle as her head, his penis, two feet from her head, was clearly visible beneath his shuka. She spluttered, choking on her delicately held tea and sank back into the interior of the car.

I had never witnessed such bedlam in a game reserve before. The cowboy, in his faded kikoi wrap, having refreshed his gin and tonic, was sitting on his car roof, eating a sandwich. It was penga, completely bloody penga, and across the river, where the cars were still arranged in considerate lines, the warden had driven away.

**PAGE 242**  *A column of white-bearded wildebeest wends its way over a hill.*

**PAGES 244/245**  *John Masefield sought 'a tall ship and a star to steer her by'. A sickle moon, a lone tent on a plain and Maasai around the fire satiated our desire.*

**PAGES 246/247**  *A breeding herd of elephant beneath a rainy-season sky.*

**PAGE 249, BELOW & THIS PAGE, ABOVE**  *The long-standing Newland and Tarlton Safari Company is currently owned by Don Young, a passionate historian who styles his safari on the early travels of Burton and Speke and, together with Daniel Kashu and Daniel Parmat, still guides his expeditions himself.*

**OPPOSITE**  *The white-bearded wildebeest migration crosses the Mara River.*

**FOLLOWING SPREAD**  *The young Maasai moran askaris and guides and their fire-circling dance, at the Newland and Tarlton camp, were as exotic to us as the ritual safari dining-table seemed to them.*

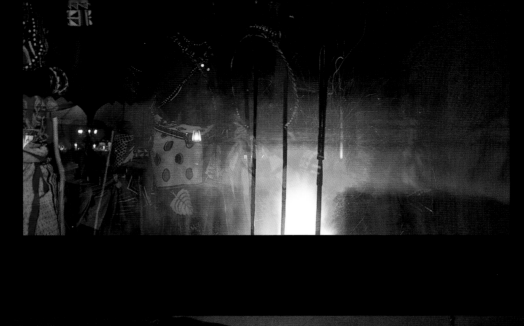

# SURVIVING CHAOS

*'I don't much care for coincidences. There is something spooky about them; you sense momentarily what it*
*must be like to live in an ordered, God-run universe, with Himself looking over your shoulder and helpfully dropping*
*coarse hints about a cosmic plan. I prefer to feel that things are chaotic, free-wheeling, permanently as well as*
*temporarily crazy – to feel the certainty of human ignorance, brutality and folly.'* Julian Barnes

I am awakened by a rush of sound. The night is absolutely dark and for a few moments my sleep-fogged mind, like a swimmer bowled over by a wave, struggles for orientation. It is raining. The falling drops are a sharp tattoo on the taut canvas of the tent which grows loud and then soft as the first windblown sheets of rain are driven ahead of the main body of the squall.

It rains like that here on the equatorial savannas of Africa. In the daylight you can watch the great squalls building, sucking up the heat and the moisture of the land, the tumult of the towering white heads turning to dark steel grey at their bases. Briefly the wind rushes towards them, plucking the loose leaves from the trees in the valleys and bending all the tall grasses of the plains in the same direction. And then all of the sky grows grey and heavy and the light is shut out, so that the land becomes sombre and suppressed and dull.

At the heart of the squall the rain begins to fall and you can smell it across the colourless, waiting land and it smells somehow of both hope and fear and you can sense it in the pit of you. The rain falls in a sheer grey wall that swallows whole ridges at a time, but at the edges, where the rain falls more thinly, it appears as a gossamer gauze drawn between the land and the sky. The storm's drift pulls the rain like a single heavy theatre curtain across the set of the land, its base dragging across the surface, curving back towards the direction it has come.

The first drops are fat and heavy and land with a bursting splat that holds no ambiguity, no reticence and one hunches one's shoulders and draws in one's neck and watches the lightless grey curtain drawing closer, knowing there is no escape.

It was raining like that now and, shrugging deeper into the blankets, I drifted back to sleep as the squall hit and the rain fell in rivulets from the canvas roof. When I awoke the rain had passed, but intermittent light drips fell with a soft tap from the branches above to remind me that I had not been dreaming. It was still dark, at least an hour before dawn, but even without groping for the luminous face of our cheap trading-store alarm clock, I knew intuitively that it was time. I fumbled around the wash-stand beside the bed for matches, found them and, striking one, held it up to the candle.

The flame of the match caught on the wick. It grew smaller as it ate down its short length and then, tasting the wax, stretched tall again. I leaned back on the frame of the bedstead. I liked waking like that. The world quiet outside, smelling wet, the drips from the leaves falling soft on the canvas. The light of the candle warm and bright enough to see the period writing desk in the far corner of the tent, but not too bright to hurt my eyes.

The rain in the night had made the morning cold and I was stamping my feet into my boots on the veranda when Daniel Logorok appeared through the trees. His bright red-and-blue-checked Maasai shuka, drawn cape-like around his body, was colourless in the dark.

'Sopa, Daniel,' I said, the Maasai greeting unfamiliar on my tongue.

'Sopa.'

'Baridi?'

'Eeh, baridi sana.'

'And wet,' I said, seeing the water on his bare calves in the faint light of the candle.

'Coffee?' he asked, producing a green and silver Thermos from under his shuka.

'Ndiyo, asante.'

And then, with a quick flourish, he wrapped his shuka tight around his otherwise naked body and, turning, walked back to the unseen fire through the dark, dripping trees.

**ABOVE**  *Rain clouds, the lure of a million animals, billow over a lone impala.*

**OPPOSITE**  *A Rüppell's griffon feeds on a casualty of the Mara River crossing.*

**PAGE 256, ABOVE**  *A crocodile pursues swimming wildebeest.*

Paler patches were just beginning to show in a cloud-streaked sky as we rolled out of camp with all the windows up and the heater on, hunched forward towards its growing warmth. I had the lights on but a thin mist hung over the ground and reflected the lights back, so I switched them off. Water in the track squished out from the tyres and, in a flat patch with some deep ruts, I felt the back of the vehicle yaw and slip with a bump into the ruts. We idled forward.

Only a few hundred metres out of camp, we saw what we thought was a jackal crossing the plain towards the river. Coming slowly closer we realised it was too big for a jackal and I cut the motor and rolled to a stop. It was a leopard, the first we had seen. He stopped and watched us, easing his body close to the ground. It was still too dark to take pictures and so, for a time, we watched each other, the leopard a black profile against the thin mist, his body held low, tense, his legs bent, half cocked and his tail out behind him, its tip curled characteristically forward.

His head was turned towards us and although I could not make out his face I could feel him watching us. Time froze, caught, drawn out and held still by the tension, the waiting, the anticipation. Then holding his chest only centimetres above the ground in that beguiling, dangerous, beautiful liquid grace that made me yearn to be him, he flowed across the last hundred metres of the plain and into the riverine trees.

I watched him to the last. I let him go and then sat still, looking out into the mist. Only when the feeling was dying, when I became aware of the morning and the cold again, did I sit back in my seat and start the car.

Mist lay on the plains so I headed for the first hill outside the camp, a low, rock-topped rise between two rivers from where one could scan the surrounding country. The black earth of the track was waterlogged from the rain, and slick and smooth as glass. The wheels spun as we climbed, the rear of the Land Rover occasionally sliding wide of the track before twisting straight again. Thick glutinous globs of mud were thrown up past the windows and stuck to the mirrors and handles of the doors.

Just before we crested the hill, a breeding herd of elephants appeared on the ridge, walking slowly down its length. Behind them a gap in the silvered layers of the clouds revealed the first orange light of dawn and, throwing the windows open to the cold, we began to work furiously. Each time the elephants approached too closely, I backed further down the hill, keeping them in silhouette against the brightening sky. Eventually, though, our backs were against the forest and we watched the elephants walk into the trees, 500 metres from where the leopard had found sanctuary.

Cameras, lenses and spent film lay scattered between us.

'Coffee?' Beverly offered, and we drank it scalding hot with our hands wrapped around the mugs and, although the sky was growing grey and threatening rain, I felt good and happy.

Slowly, without pressure, we sorted out the chaos of cameras and then, as we finished our coffee, Beverly glassed the side of the hill down which the elephants had come. She paused for a time at one point then, handing me the binoculars, pointed out a Thomson's gazelle she thought was behaving strangely. It looked as if it might be wanting to give birth. Holding the last of my coffee in one hand and driving in a wide semi-circle, we approached it circumspectly with the dull light of the grey dawn behind us.

The grass of the hillside was short, cropped to spiky tufts by the thousands of wildebeest of the migration. For now, only a few could be seen, perhaps a hundred, scattered mostly over the plain below. I could hear the 'gnu' call of the bulls through the open windscreen. Looking through the binoculars at a distance of several hundred metres, I could see the gazelle clearly and it was plain that she was having convulsions of some sort.

Angling at a point obliquely past her and letting the motor idle, we painstakingly slowly closed the distance between ourselves and her. If this was a birth it would be a first for us. We have seen births before but either just afterwards, or halfway through, or obscured by grass or trees. Never like this, out in the open from the very start. Our progress was horribly slow, too slow. I knew that wild births often happen in a rush and with each passing second our chances were slipping away.

In a particularly wet section I felt the back of the Land Rover sliding out and, fearful that the sudden movement might spook her, I reluctantly applied the brakes, engaged low range, and crept forward even more slowly. The line between success and failure, between being close enough to work and not spooking her, or of her giving birth first, was growing taut. Subconsciously I was clenching the muscles of my jaw and, like watching a child wind a guitar string too tight, I was aware of the rising note of the tension, unsure when it would snap.

At just more than a hundred metres away, I thought she tried to stand and, cursing once, I killed the motor. We sat rigidly still but she remained where she was and then, moving in exaggerated slow motion, we lifted our cameras and brought them to bear.

With the naked eye she was still a little too far away, but through the telephoto lens and binoculars we could see her clearly. She lay on her side with her belly toward us. I could see her legs go stiff and straight as

the convulsions gripped her. I watched fascinated as each one passed and, as her body went soft again, her delicate black tongue licked her lips and the tip of her nose in a gesture of calming, of self assurance. She was gripped by a mighty spasm that forced her free legs ramrod straight and something black appeared by her rump. The head of the foal was free.

We were just too far away to get good pictures. We needed to be 20 metres closer. I knew that it could ruin the situation, but I was convincing myself that it would be worth a try when I heard the alarm snort of

two or three wildebeest together. Looking out to my right I could see them, heads held up, alert, and stamping their feet as they snorted. For a while I searched for the cause of their concern but could see nothing, and then further away from where I had been concentrating, closer towards us, I saw a yellow form moving across the hillside. It was a hyaena running in that lazy lope that at first glance seems almost incidental, casual, and yet is deceptively swift.

It was running in a straight line, seemingly directly towards us. The hyaena in the Masai Mara have learnt that vehicles often stop beside something of interest, a kill perhaps, or a carcass, and in the early morning investigating a stationary vehicle can be as productive as watching vultures. I knew that in approaching us it would come too close to the birth. Its nose would detect it; the smell of the blood, the afterbirth, the wet foal. That would spoil everything. Damning our luck, I started the Land Rover and swung away up the hill.

The hyaena ignored us, running straight by on a course that would take it within 50 metres of the gazelle. We started to change lenses in preparation for the inevitable action. When the hyaena was still 250 metres away, the gazelle surprised me completely. She got to her feet and trotted lightly out of the hyaena's path, the head of the foal protruding out of her rump.

A small herd of Thomson's gazelle was grazing on the hillside close to where we had stopped and she trotted to within 30 metres of us to be among them and they turned to watch the hyaena. It loped straight on and she bent to nibble some of the short sweet grass. Only when the hyaena was out of sight did she walk away from the group, but her troubles were not over yet.

A young male Thomson's gazelle, fascinated by the scent of the birth, and probably by the pheromones and hormones it released, followed her away from the group. He walked around her, followed, sniffing at her rump and drawing his upper lip back in a hormone-induced grimace, and then began walking with his forelegs straight and stiff, which in

the rut is a prelude to mating. It was funny at first and I wanted to chuckle and to tell him he was too young, that he had it all wrong, that he was making a fool of himself, but I could not and, as he persisted, my frustration grew.

For more than 25 minutes he followed and pestered her with his attentions. Each time he came too close she trotted another 10 metres away, the head of the foal bumping at her rump. Twice she managed to lie down, but before anything could begin he arrived again and she got up and moved off. Each time I groaned inwardly with mounting anguish.

The contact call of the male Thomson's gazelle is at the best of times pathetic. It is a thin, wheezing, drawn-out bleat and sounds weak and pleading and afraid. I railed against it now as he followed her yet again, calling.

'Dumb bastard,' I muttered, and sat hard on the urge to drive in and chase the fool away.

Finally, when my exasperation was so extended that I felt the urge to weep, he turned from her and trotted back to the group where we had remained.

For a while she stood quite still and looked about. She nibbled compulsively at the grass and then looked again. About 50 metres from the track we had followed up the hill, she lay down. I started the vehicle and worked my way towards her. At 60 metres from her she still showed no agitation at our presence and we stopped and set up.

The contractions came quickly now and, through the lens, I could watch them ripple down the black line of her belly fur. The shoulders of the foal appeared, shiny in their coating of placenta. Sometimes the contractions started again before the previous one had finished and I watched mesmerised as just the tip of her hoof arched, quivering forward on her already stiff leg, like a ballerina compelled unwittingly to a final moment of grace in this wild, terrible, wondrous dance.

With about two thirds of the body of the foal out it became stuck against the ground behind her. She pushed, but it was wedged there and did not move. She reached her head back between her hind legs and licked at its face. It shook its oversized ears and, in the movement of mother and foal, it became unwedged and the hind legs of the foal came out in a rush. It was free, born, and we had seen it all.

With its legs bent beneath it and covered in the placenta, the foal shuffled forward between the mother's hind legs and lay close against her belly. She licked its big ears, under its chin, along its back and at its rump. As she licked, the translucent veined covering of the placenta

came away and the curly wet fur started to dry. Between her hind legs the gazelle came across the afterbirth and ate it like a piece of spaghetti, chewing it with a sideways motion of her jaw and licking constantly at her lips with the unfamiliar taste.

Soon the foal tried to stand. Its legs were gangly and long and it pitched forward onto its nose or wobbled backwards and sat down in an uncharacteristic squat. It fell against its mother and tripped over her legs. At one point, as she licked at its belly, it took a step forward for balance and her licking lifted it clear of the ground, pitch-poling it over her neck. Within half an hour it was standing, legs splayed.

In the distance I heard two plovers venting their annoyance. I looked up and saw a jackal trotting down the track towards us. The plovers were dive-bombing it, shrieking as they stooped. The mother saw it too and, breaking off the fawn's suckling, moved a few paces. The fawn made to follow her but she trotted hastily away and instead it lay down. The mother moved towards the distant group of Thomson's gazelle and the fawn put its chin on the ground and lowered its ears to the damp earth.

Lying flat and still was a remarkable camouflage. Even from close proximity the fawn appeared as little more than an insignificant smudge on the open vista of the plain, a tussock or a clod that would draw no attention. I marvelled that lying absolutely still was so ingrained and successful a survival technique. It was the unwritten rule of instinct, the buried, incontestable knowledge of evolution rooted in the genes of the newborn. Even in the face of extreme danger, a cheetah hunting where it knew fawns had been hidden, I had seen it succeed. Those that moved, died. The jackal trotted right past the prostrate fawn and, even though it circled curiously around us, the fawn remained unmoving and the jackal did not see it and trotted away.

It had happened, it was over, and I sat back from my camera. We had seen it, photographed it and we had not changed its course. The sun was breaking through the clouds, fragmenting them as we moved away towards the Mara River where we hoped the wildebeest would be massing to cross towards the rain.

In the afternoon the storms had grown again like gigantic mushrooms over the land. Vast explosions of clouds that advanced menacingly from the horizons, growing swollen and ugly and turning from white to purple and then black. When the rain started to fall the other vehicles had fled, but we stayed through it and watched the roads become rivers and the animals turn their backs to the onslaught. It was after sunset when we climbed away from the river towards the camp, wet and cramped and full of the day.

It was still raining lightly and the track back to the camp ran with water. The hard black earth of the track was so slippery that I could turn the wheel and have no effect for five metres or more. The Land Rover slid and spun but kept rolling forward. Mud flew up so thickly from the tyres that the vehicle was almost black. There was no point in trying to avoid the holes and the ruts; we just slid into them and the windshield wipers slapped at the muddy water that was sprayed up over the bonnet. It was prematurely dark well before we neared the camp.

We were coming down the hill where we had seen the elephants in the morning, driving slowly, not using the brakes and letting the engine hold our speed. Ahead of me, almost exactly where we had witnessed the birth of the gazelle, I thought I saw the bright reflection of eyes in the headlights. I looked again as the wipers swept the windscreen clean. I was not mistaken. I could not make out a body, but definitely eyes, low to the ground on the ridge right in the middle of the tracks. There was nothing I could do, we were too close; even with the brakes we would slide at least another 10 metres past it. I killed the motor and the lights. I touched my foot gently on the brake so that we would slow just a touch but not slide. Blind, we trundled forward into the night.

In the long, stretched-out seconds I recalled the morning, of all that had been survived, of the instinct to lie low and still. I knew nothing could prepare the foal for this and I hoped Beverly was praying. I could feel the surface of the road on the tyres through the steering wheel under my hands. Without my eyes, all my senses had tuned to my ears and to touch. I could hear and feel through the tips of my fingers and the soles of my feet, the splashing of the water in the track, the patter of rain on the roof and I waited for the soft dull thunk of flesh against unyielding steel. The silence stretched on. I was holding my breath, straining my nerve ends, helplessly sure of what must come. Thirty metres further on, the Land Rover finally stopped. I dropped my head against the steering wheel and closed my eyes with relief.

**PAGE 259**  *A hippopotamus becomes surrounded by a deluge of wildebeest.*

**PAGES 260/261**  *Thwarted by a steep bank after crossing the Mara River, wildebeest wait their turn for the narrow path out.*

**ABOVE**  *With the quiet of a butterfly, a leopard flits through the wooded valleys of the Masai Mara.*

**LEFT**  *The swift current of the rain-swollen Mara River draws the columns of the migration downstream.*

**PAGE 264, ABOVE**  *Mating lions. Masai Mara;*
**BELOW**  *The choked banks of a crossing. Mara River.*

**PAGE 265, ABOVE**  *Mud encrusted, a lone buffalo scents the air in the mature fever-tree forest of Lake Nakuru;*
**BELOW**  *A cheetah defends its kill. Masai Mara.*

**THIS & FOLLOWING SPREAD**  *Lake Nakuru National Park, its entrance gate at the end of a street in Nakuru town, is one of Kenya's smaller reserves and yet supports a remarkable host of wildlife, including white rhinoceros and lion. The ruby in its crown, however, are the flocks of flamingos that stalk its shallow shore and the flights of pelicans that come to roost in its sanctuary.*

# AMBOSELI, TSAVO EAST & WEST

We, like Hemingway, like the Queen of England, like Selous, like Rebmann, have seen the snows of Kilimanjaro. The question is: will you? It is one of Africa's singular landmarks, the snowy peak seen from a distance across the border in Kenya's Amboseli National Park, with giraffe or elephant in the foreground. And now even that view is as tenuous as snow on the equator for, in an illegal act in 2005, President Kibaki of Kenya deproclaimed Amboseli as a national park.

The snows of Kilimanjaro are melting. Fast. You may dismiss me as summarily as the learned members of the Royal Geographical Society dismissed the missionary Johan Rebmann's 1849 report of permanent snow on a mountain in Africa within a few degrees of the equator. 'Preposterous,' they said, 'of evidence of snow in the vicinity of the equator, there is not one jot.'

As the travel writer Philip Briggs suggests, it seems remarkable that they so perfunctorily chose to dismiss that claim and did not venture to question its authenticity with the traders of the African coast at the time. The traders' caravans routinely penetrated the African interior and would undoubtedly have known of Kilimanjaro. Rebmann had to wait 12 years for the experienced geologist Von der Decken to uphold his claim.

In 12 years you will probably still catch a glimpse of the white peak, but in our lifetime, ours, the snows of Kilimanjaro will be gone. Carbon emissions, the future of the ozone layer, global warming, the greenhouse effect – it is too late to put the brakes on our selfish carelessness.

'Preposterous,' I thought. Not something that my doing is really affecting, we will catch it in time. Climate change does not come about in decades, I thought, it is an evolution, and now I see that evolution has accelerated into the scope of a lifetime. It does not leave much room for apathy.

Yet it is a pall of apathy that I sense most strongly when I consider the land to the north and east of Mount Kilimanjaro.

The flat, arid country of Amboseli, the red-earth thorn scrub of Tsavo East and the rocky hills of Tsavo West. A pervasive apathy, an apathy that has closed its eyes to the reality of its demons so that, like a child too scared to climb from its bed, it has reached the proportions of monsters. An apathy in which the red sand of Kenya's time is slipping through its hands.

It is an apathy born of the pompous, blind to the truth, a belief that the colonial legacy of the national parks is an irrevocable certitude. The unconsidered certainty of conviction that the wilderness, its heroes, adventurers and people are so much a part of Kenya's history that it cannot be undone. It is an attitude that avoids the truth, a comfortable ignorance that allows backs to be turned, to shrug it off. To leave it for the next generation to fight. And now Amboseli as a national park is gone.

What is the future for this tiny 392 square kilometres of land that is the quintessential image of Africa, given by a quisling president to the local Maasai council? I would like to hope, but I am tempered by my knowledge of apathy.

Amboseli is one of Kenya's most visited parks, generating considerable fees. In its new state it must therefore too be considered within the parameters of Kenya's national apathy towards gravy-train governance. A routine acceptance of a corrupt, burgeoning civil service where brothers, uncles and distant cousins find employment and where governance monies are sidetracked, misappropriated or just plain disappear. Will the Maasai of this arid, salty plain, with its marsh of elephant and buffalo, be able to use their fierce wit to ensure fairness, or will they prove to be all too human, like the rest of us, kept ignorant by those we trust?

Sometimes it is difficult to know who to trust. Occasionally there are more sinister forces at play where an apathy exists. Forces whose persuasions betray what one knows in one's heart, what one feels in one's gut. Forces whose persuasion is the corruption of fear, the knowledge of guns.

**ABOVE & FOLLOWING SPREAD** *The barren, arid country surrounding Amboseli is a Maasai heartland.*

**OPPOSITE** *From the vantage of a granite koppie, a young lion looks out over the Tsavo River valley. Tsavo West.*

I saw its work in Tsavo, where 31 000 elephant were killed between 1975 and 1991. But Tsavo means 'place of slaughter' and the killing is not done. You can feel it as you drive through the land. The way a lion runs, in its eyes the same terror as a bus station mongrel beaten too many times. The great void of the land, quiet, with no tracks in the sand, just the palms and the river and the rocks and the sun. The wild, flared nostrils of a buffalo that wanted to charge, that stamped the ground and would not drink because he had our scent on the wind. There are animals there – some. There are the scouts, too, with their epaulettes and their dark green four-wheel drives clustered around the entrance gates or driving fast to some other side. There is the national road, from Nairobi to Mombasa, which divides the parks into east and west. It cuts the 19 000 square-kilometre wilderness almost in half, but it erodes it far more than that. It brings loops of wire and firearms.

We had arrived late one evening at the Mombasa Highway entrance gate to the Tsavo West Park, delayed by a mechanical repair in Voi. The scout refused to let us in as it was too far to reach a campsite before dark. Finally, he had capitulated on condition that we sleep there at the gate. We had driven about 250 metres from the gate to a small clearing. The scout had arrived, running, his eyes wide with fright. 'We could not sleep there. No, no, no! Men would come in the night.' I wanted to know what men, but he would not answer, just insisted that we camp in his compound, beside his hut.

The night was uneventful, as calm as the day, except that the scout carried his weapon with him all the time. We departed at first light and followed the palm-lined Tsavo River into a singular country of bouldered outcroppings and scattered baobabs. We got lost and emerged hours later at the rhinoceros sanctuary, which was closed. The road to Mzima

Springs climbed into a land of rocky hills and, threading through some narrow passages, emerged into a network of pretty valleys where the lodges were set against their sides. There were streams and dams and animals too.

Mzima Springs, which lay to the west, was an oasis-like paradise, unlike anything else in Africa. A crystal torrent gushed from the volcanic earth into fever tree-fringed pools, teeming with hippopotamus, crocodile and fish. We had, on leaving the springs, followed a bad, rocky, eroded road beside the springs down the valley. It led to a place where all that pristine wonderland was led into a pipe. Sucked dry. Not one drop passing by, so that the valley below and the valley above were two different worlds. I saw from my map that the water pipeline led to the dusty, unkempt town of Voi.

I recalled that the mechanic in Voi, who had done our repair in his open workshop beside the road, had turned on the tap and let it run in a rivulet onto the dry red sand. He had put his head under it, cupped it in his hand and spat it out. He had encouraged me to drink. 'It's pure, good!' and I remember it now, remember standing there and watching it run.

**ABOVE** *Buffalo graze on a plain whose porous volcanic crust gathers the crystal waters of Mzima Springs. Tsavo West.*

**OPPOSITE** *Elephant and Mount Kilimanjaro. Amboseli.*

**PREVIOUS SPREAD**  *On a quiet reach of the Tsavo River, where it passes through a singular country of eroded rocky hills, an elephant cow reacts to our scent. Tsavo East.*

**ABOVE**  *Doum palms frame a vervet monkey eating fallen fruit. Tsavo West.*

**LEFT**  *Bushbuck. Tsavo West.*

**OPPOSITE**  *Elephant dust-bathing. Amboseli.*

**THIS SPREAD** *The clear waters of Mzima Springs offer an Aladdin's cave view of a seldom-seen world. Tsavo West.*

279

**TOP** *A mature Grant's gazelle's horns reach almost fictional proportions; the Rowland Ward record is 31.5 inches. Tsavo East.*

**MIDDLE** *The red sand of Tsavo rouges the skin of the elephants there.*

**ABOVE** *An eroding koppie. Tsavo West.*

**OPPOSITE** *The tight, heavy power of a lone Tsavo East buffalo bull.*

**FOLLOWING SPREAD** *Looking away from Mount Kilimanjaro, an Amboseli sunrise reveals a distant grazing herd of zebra and wildebeest.*

# RWANDA

## Parc Des Volcans & Mgahinga

# PARC DES VOLCANS & MGAHINGA

In looking back down upon where I had stood looking up, I pause. The scenery is different, splendid, high equatorial Africa where volcanic peaks rise from a mist-softened landscape of round green hills, but my view is the same. I carry it with me in my head and, despite the strong influence of the pristine forest through which we have been climbing, I cannot shake its melancholy.

In truth, the forest probably endorses it, for the forest is the land in its natural state. Its tall, mature trees, whose trunks beneath the high canopy crowd the earth even on the steepest slopes, so that every view is reduced to a glimpse framed between them, faceted small windows onto the world below. Green is pervasive, the colour of the light filtered through the canopy. A diffused cast that reaches into the shadow and falls upon your skin, that tints brown and black and yellow until it seems that you can sense it in your nostrils as strongly as the odour of the damp, rich earth that breaks open beneath your feet.

It is the primary colour of the riotous undergrowth that blankets the forest floor. The kind of undergrowth I imagined Robinson Crusoe to have encountered when, as a child, I invented a fantasy country in my head, playing with a crude wooden sword in a stand of bamboo in a friend's garden. We slash at it now as we did then, cutting a path with bright-edged machetes through leaves and stems and vines. Leaves the size of dinner plates with prickly hairy surfaces, narrow curving leaves with purple margins, serrated-edged leaves transparently thin with minute red veins like those you see in a heavy drinker's face. Leaves that couch a tiny blue flower, leaves eaten by caterpillars and elephants, pale lime leaves still softly folded in the newness of their birth. We slash at them and leave them discarded in our wake, wiping the sweat of our effort from our faces.

We have come to see the mountain gorillas and after climbing high up the sides of Bisoke, one of Rwanda's volcanic peaks, we have left the narrow footpath and are following the contour of the mountain, cutting our way through. We are close but have not found them yet and have paused to listen and catch our breath. One of our fellow climbers indicates the tracker we occasionally glimpse a distance ahead and asks the guide sitting with us if he has found them yet.

The guide talks softly into his hand-held radio. There is a crackle of static, a pause, and then a voice talking quietly gives a one-sentence answer. The guide looks up, 'nothing yet to see'.

I am arrested by his reply. Am I just here to see, only to see? What do I mean, what does he mean by see, is it the same? Is seeing to look and to look alone? What of the feeling of my fingers in the damp, soft earth, is that not part of what I see?

I think back on my wanting to be here. Did I imagine that gathering an image in my camera and my head to carry away would be sufficient, or was there more? Was there less? Was it just something to be done, to be counted, ticked and then to move on? What was my desire, what lay in my heart as I looked up at this mountain from down below?

Through a stained-glass window-shaped opening between the trees, I can see down to the valleys below and, in looking down, I feel the stirrings of my melancholy. Gradually, softly, like falling asleep, my thoughts move from the outward scene to within my head. My eyes are open but they are still, turned inward, looking at myself, at my melancholy, for I know that somewhere in that worry, in that sadness, lies what I truly came to find.

We had driven into Rwanda on a back road, an impeccably tarred, neatly marked, new back road. The result, I surmised, of the aid that had poured into the country in the wake of the Hutu–Tutsi genocide. A

**OPPOSITE, BELOW** *A youth carries fodder from the compact, fertile fields on the slopes of the Virungas.*

**PAGE 284** *The Virunga Massif is not a range of mountains, but a series of eroded volcanic peaks.*

genocide it seems that the Rwandans would rather forget and are reluctant to talk about. There were few vehicles on the road, but it was rampant with pedestrians who were punctuated by the occasional bell-ringing cyclist bearing seemingly impossible loads. Never had I seen such a constant stream of people in so rural a setting. Both verges were filled to the capacity of a city sidewalk. Houses, stalls, informal vendors, cycle-repair venues and barber shops lined its edge in densities way beyond the average urban suburbia.

In looking over the country, it seemed that every square inch was attended. Small clusters of houses stood everywhere and, to the far horizon, every nook and every cranny that had not been built on had been parcelled into small, neat agricultural patches that were worked with intensity. I had looked past them to the forested slopes and peaks of the Virungas and wondered how long they could stand in the face of such human pressure. What chance they stood in the rule of need and desire.

The volcanic peaks of the Virungas fall at the junction of three countries, Rwanda, Uganda and the Democratic Republic of the Congo, and are protected in each by parks, but the parks are small and, combined, form only 470 square kilometres of protected area. More that half of that lies in the Democratic Republic of the Congo, which has been in a state of anarchy long enough for the condition of its park and its inhabitants to be entirely uncertain.

'Borderline,' I had thought. This final small strip of mountain gorilla country was borderline both in its position and tenuous frangibility. Propped up by money. It was a horrible thought, depressing, and it made me sad. I do not believe in money, not that I am blind to its power, but I know that, although many work for it, foot soldiers do not go to war for it. Perhaps that was what I hoped to find, what I had come here to

see. Just what other ingredient was cause enough to give the mountain gorilla its due.

I tore a strip of rotten bark from the log beneath me and held it under my nose, inhaling deeply. It smelt musty and rich, like mushrooms, and reminded me of something that would not quite come to mind. Fishing, perhaps, with worms in a stream, the tin in which they wriggled smelt much the same. And suddenly in mid-inhale I stopped, rigid, for the answer was plain.

I remembered standing on the bridge looking down into the crystal stream. The line was still coiled in my hand, the worms still safe in the tin. The trailings of a weed crossed by the current swept over the pebbled bottom and then, in the corner of my vision, without stealth, but quickly, a trout swung out from behind a stone to swallow a drifting nymph and then returned to its hidden lair in the shadow. I watched the arc of its tail and it was as if a wolf had howled at the moon.

The world in that instant had changed. Pretty before, it had been touched by a spark, become alive, electric, filled with wonder and promise. It had become complete. I had felt it since in many things. The smell of woodsmoke on my clothes, walking to the sighing of a breeze in the trees, a hyaena's call at dusk, the way a wild dog runs. It is when one's spirit sees. I was on this mountain for that, more than anything. It was the elixir to my melancholy, for it is when the spirit sees that we truly perceive and know and become possessed and can love and fight and remember and cherish and see something for its full worth. I stood and shouldered my pack and, while the others rested, I walked to the front, peering into the shadowed realm, eager for my first glimpse of those amber eyes, eager to set myself aflame.

**TOP** *Our guide, Fidele Nsengiyumva, watches a silverback gorilla.*

**PAGE 288** *High-altitude bamboo forests are a favoured haunt of mountain gorillas, the fresh young stems a delicacy.*

**PAGE 289, ABOVE** *Cute? Food? Powerful medicine? Or the tenuous hope for the severely endangered?;* **BELOW** *Gorillas feed above the small crater lake of Bisoke Peak. Rwanda.*

# ALAIN'S DEATH

The madman is babbling at me. I do not yet know that he is a madman although I am beginning to suspect it. He turns away, walking a few paces, muttering, as if composing his thoughts and then turns back on his heel and continues his tirade in what I presume is a concoction of French and the local dialect. I understand not one word and shrug once again for his benefit, but he continues to address me without a pause.

The day is on the cusp between twilight and dawn and I am glad to make out only a few scattered clouds clinging to the heights of the peaks. I am early, too early, and it is only the madman and me alone in the chill, looking down on the fog-shrouded valleys below, waiting. A child appears on the red earth road that runs straight and slippery from yesterday's rain between two rows of tall, straight trees. He stops to watch the spectacle I make with the madman who is warming to his oratory now and starting to emphasise his speech with his hands. The child remains still, rooted to the spot where he stopped, his face expressionless, watching, just watching, a soft-cover school exercise book with yellowed and bent corners, clutched across his chest.

The first honeyed light of the sun strikes the tips of the peaks and, stamping the cold from my legs, I walk over to the Land Rover where Beverly sits swaddled in jackets, her hands still around a now empty mug, and fetch a camera. The madman follows. The metal of the camera is warm from the interior of the vehicle but quickly grows cold against my fingers. I find a rock on which to support it and start to compose my pictures. The madman starts to talk again and, without lifting my eye from the camera, I raise my hand for him to stop. I am surprised when he does, abruptly, in mid-stride, like a needle ripped from a record. For a time there is only the clicking of the shutter in the wash of silence that follows.

From the road I become aware of a soft murmuring. More children have arrived, but I keep my back to them and work on. Growing slowly bolder, they draw closer until one of them breaks the silence.

' 'allo, Monsieur, what is yoh nome?'

It is a chorus I have heard a hundred times before and, knowing that it seldom goes further, I raise my hand for their silence too, but this merely incites them and several more voices join the chant. Suddenly the madman looms big in the lens as he rushes in front of the camera and grabs a stick lying on the ground. He raises the stick and charges the children who laugh and scatter, scampering easily out of his way across the damp, short grass of the hillside. Their taunts turn to him and, for a moment, he turns wildly on the spot with his stick raised above his head, unsure which of his tormentors to chase, but when he bends and picks up a small rock, they run. He turns to me and smiles and, when I grin back, he breaks out into a laugh. A laugh of triumph, of a job well done. For the rest of the morning he ignores the stick and randomly picks up stones which he tosses up and catches again, chuckling afresh each time he does so. The stones are wet and muddy and he wipes the mud from his hands on his threadbare clothes, occasionally across his face. It makes him look more wild, more mad, but his demeanour has softened.

There is some activity now, a red vehicle has arrived to park beside ours and someone is sweeping the path to the visitors' centre. We still have time, however, and, as the sun etches a crisp line of light high on the face of the mountains, I look up from the cold, shadowed foothills to where we must climb.

Because the foothills are already part of a high country, the peaks are close and seem to me not as awe inspiring or impressive as other mountains I have known. Right to their very tops they are swathed in the luxuriant growth of the tropics and only Mikeno Peak raises a sheer basalt massif against the sky. They do not form a range but rise as scattered individuals through the foothills, and it is only when I see them for what they are that they become transformed, and my gaze lingers as my thoughts run across their face and pause on the once fiery, now quiet volcanoes. Time has so eroded them that most are steep-sided fragments of their original upheaval and only one retains a distinctive cone-like shape.

As the sun reaches down towards the apex of the clustered rural houses, the sounds of the valley's waking gradually swell; a cow calls for its calf in a series of low, drawn-out bawls, a woman shouts a child's name several times before it answers, I hear kindling being broken and, over the soft strokes of the man sweeping the path, a crow is cawing from the branches above where we are waiting. The door of the red car beside us opens and a silver-haired man steps out, but he is dressed too lightly for the cold and, slapping his arms, he climbs back into the vehicle. The sun's warmth is releasing the scent of the dew and the fragrance of the pines into the air. The madman chuckles and hefts a stone at the crow.

I am chafing to be gone, to be climbing into this cold beautiful morning, to feel the bite of my pack and the beads of perspiration on my forehead, to savour the cool, damp air of the forest as it passes over my tongue and teeth and to thrill to that private euphoria of walking in a wild, still place on the opening petals of the day.

It is some time, though, before we are assigned to a group. Three other South Africans, a couple and a youth, whom I wrongly assume to be their

*'Clear-eyed, as from some mountain pool, What other gaze*
*The all-but-vanished innocence still, Face to face, Like living memory*
*Stares through whoever stands, Near-blinded in its place?'* Peter Sacks, 2007

son, a Rwandan who says almost nothing except when you press him to, and the silver-haired man from the red car, who introduces himself as Alain from Belgium.

Alain's disposition is as he appears, soft with an inclination to the cheerful, and when our guide, Fidele Nsengiyumva, who speaks good French but only a little English, discovers Alain to be fluent in both, he quickly assigns him the task of communicator, a responsibility to which Alain warms with humour. Alain's silver hair makes him appear older than he is and, although he is paunchy, his optimistic disposition gives him a youthful air and I am quick to like him.

Driving our own vehicles, we follow Fidele to the starting point. The country roads in Rwanda are narrow, meandering between fields and clusters of mud-brick houses whose walls stand so close to the road that we can sometimes touch them through the windows. Ours are the only vehicles I see, but a steady stream of pedestrians and cyclists overloaded with bulging sacks of potatoes keeps our progress slow. At one point water has eroded a gully, deep enough to swallow our Land Rover, right beside the road. An approaching group of musicians in orange shirts, with an electric guitar, an amplifier and a set of drums on their heads, are forced to the edge of the gully and I see them looking nervously into the hole as they wait for us to edge past, their equipment swaying on their heads.

The road climbs higher and higher towards the base of Bisoke Peak. In the steep sections, it has been roughly cobbled with small boulders against which the vehicle jars and rolls. It is a relief when we finally arrive at the starting point and step out into the now warm sun.

Fidele offers us stout sticks. Alain accepts one and taps it against his leg and it is then that I notice his shoes. They are flat-soled slip-ons, more suited to a stroll across a mall than a hike up a mountain, and I grow concerned about how the unfolding morning will be. My concerns are well founded but in the course of the day, Alain's shoes will be the least of them.

We set off in single file on a narrow path between tightly terraced fields. Our party has swelled to include two armed soldiers and a porter. One of the soldiers is young. He carries his weapon in both hands across his chest and his slightly frowning expression never relaxes from the earnest. From the outset he refuses to be included in photographs. His far older companion has a benign, angular face that in moments of repose seems tinged with sadness. His weapon is slung across his back and, although he is reticent, almost reclusive in his presence, I sense in him a quiet *joie de vivre* at the prospect of a day on the mountain.

Although we have not gone far, I notice that Alain is already breathing hard and several times has to stop to catch his breath.

I am walking behind Alain and, in places where the path is still in shadow and damp, I can see his flat-soled shoes slip. I slow my pace to ease the pressure on him and gradually we fall behind.

In a grove of eucalyptus trees Fidele waits for us to catch up. He crushes the leaves and passes them between us to inhale the potent, distinctive fragrance. Alain does not translate and waves the proffered leaves away. He is leaning with both hands on his stick and breathing heavily, his face flushed. All of us notice it, it is impossible not to, and Alain notices our noticing.

Fidele sets out again, but even though his pace is markedly slower, we stop twice for Alain before reaching the first steep section. It is only a few hundred metres long and at the end of it lies the buffalo wall, the demarcation between the fields and the mountain reserve.

I am still behind Alain and I can see him willing his feet upward, he is pushing hard on the stick but his upper body is tiring. His breath is coming in gasps. When Fidele pauses, Alain sits against the steep bank, leaning forward onto the stick. I am standing below him and I see his gaze fall on the pack of cameras I am carrying and then travel wistfully to the horizon.

'Too much time behind my desk,' he says to no one in particular. 'I knew, well, I thought...' He gives a short laugh, which becomes a little spluttering cough. He dabs at his forehead and the corners of his mouth with a napkin. His face is flushed and I can see thin veins in his cheeks, fiery red.

'I thought,' Alain begins, and then stops. 'No, Belgium is flat.'

**ABOVE** *Rural house. Kisoro, Uganda.*

**PAGE 291** *Forest giants transformed into water taxis. Lake Bunyoni, Uganda.*

When we stop again, the buffalo wall is 50 metres away. Alain is looking bad, his eyes are bulging now and his chest shudders with its need for air. I am resting my pack against the ground and have been worrying that Alain's delays are spoiling our opportunities. Already the sun is too high for the soft light I was hoping for and soon the gorillas will start moving to begin their day's feeding. Now, however, I am worried about Alain. He has already pushed himself way beyond his endurance and his body seems close to convulsions. As if he can hear my thoughts, he looks me in the eye.

'I want to see them.' It is not a plea, it is a statement. 'I came right across the world, I came to see them.' And he pushes himself up on his stick.

Reaching the buffalo wall is a small victory. 'Parc National des Volcans' a small sign announces. The wall is a thick, handmade barrier of unmortared stone, raised to the height of a man's chest, that extends right around the base of the park. We pass through a narrow entrance into the unspoilt forest of the mountain; the path disappears into the thick growth, it is angling straight upwards.

We are all climbing now. The floor of the forest is damp and soft with humus and I must occasionally kick a footing to hold the weight of myself and the bulky pack. My own breath fills my ears and for a short time my thoughts leave Alain, who is now at the back. The South African youth points out a small, green chameleon and I ask Fidele to stop whilst I take some pictures. In the stillness I can hear Alain climbing towards us. He is sobbing for breath. I hear the soft voice of the porter who is with him. It sounds as if he is pulling Alain bodily up the mountain.

Alain arrives as I finish and collapses unceremoniously on the path. He is beyond caring now, his clothes are stained by greenery and mud where he has slipped and he wipes his soiled hand across his face. Despite his flushed cheeks, his face is ashen. He tries to spit but does not have the breath and the saliva clings to the side of his mouth until he wipes it away with the napkin. I look up at the path climbing steadily towards the peak and know that Alain will not make it.

Fidele makes the decision we have all known is inevitable. Gently he explains to Alain that he cannot go on. He is not physically up to what lies ahead and he is compromising the group. I think Alain has known it, as we all have. His head is lying inert in a patch of bracken, his eyes are closed and, without opening them, he nods and waves us on with his hand. Fidele tells him that the porter will stay with him.

For a long time we climb in silence. I can feel my own breath surging in and out of my chest. I am aware of the texture of the damp, rotting wood of a log I climb over, the sound of leaves scraping against my pack, that what I thought was a bird is the sound that Fidele's hand-held radio makes when he presses the transmit button, which he does compulsively. My thoughts are with Alain.

After nearly half an hour of climbing, Fidele pauses and talks at length on the radio. He finishes and stands for a while, listening. We start to traverse the mountain. I hear two soft whistles and see the trackers for the first time below and to the side of us. We join them and they lead us into a steep-sided clearing in the forest above a small crater lake.

Cutting a path with his machete, Fidele moves slowly forward. I am behind him and suddenly there is a gorilla right beside me. I catch my

pack, zip it open and begin to work, passing Beverly a camera to prompt her back from her enchantment.

This family is more habituated than other gorillas I have seen in the past and we move easily among them. At one point, a young gorilla moving through our now spread-out group comes across the South African woman and pushes her gently on the leg to move her out of the way. The gorillas avoid eye contact, but from time to time I catch one stealing a furtive, curious glance at me from under its heavy eyebrows.

I am working furiously, changing lenses, loading film, dropping one camera for another. I glance at my watch, 50 minutes have gone and I am running short of film. Fidele is standing above and beside me. I hear

breath for he is no more than a long arm stretch away, leaning back in the foliage, chewing on a celery-like stalk. I can clearly see the lashes around his red-brown eyes, the stubble on his chin. He ignores me stoically as if I were no more than a bird and chews slowly on the stalk. I move forward for the others to see and then we are among them, a family of 14 gorillas.

A large female cradles a tiny baby on her lap, two youngsters roughand-tumble with each other, crashing through the foliage down the steep slope, an adult is weaving a nest on the crest of a tree below us. I look at my watch, as our time with them is strictly limited to an hour. I lay down my

a soft whistle but can see nothing when I look and so I turn to Fidele. On his face is an expression of absolute rapture bordering on disbelief, like a child caught up in a fairytale. He is looking beyond the gorillas and it is a few seconds before I make out the porter walking through the trees into the clearing with Alain beside him.

I sit down in the foliage close to the young gorilla beside me. He has no idea of the magnitude of his aura or how far the charisma of his presence stretches out from the mountain. Fidele is smiling and nodding to himself.

**ABOVE & OPPOSITE, ABOVE**  *Mountain gorilla. Endangered. An animal is Endangered when it is not Critically Endangered but is facing a very high risk of extinction in the wild. Its numbers are estimated at less than 710;* **BELOW** *Sabinyo Peak. Kisoro, Uganda.*

**FOLLOWING SPREAD**  *The Virunga peaks stand at the junction of three countries. Bisoke Peak, Rwanda; Mikeno Peak, Central African Republic.*

## SOUTH AFRICA

### KRUGER & THE PRIVATE RESERVES

**Kruger National Park**
South African National Parks
P.O. Box 787, Pretoria 0001, South Africa
Tel: (+27-12) 428 9111; Fax: (27-12) 426 5500
E-mail: *reservations@sanparks.co.za*
*www.sanparks.org*

**Pafuri Camp – Makuleke Concession, Kruger National Park**
Wilderness Safaris
*www.wilderness-safaris.com*

**Sabi Sabi Private Game Reserve**
P.O. Box 52665, Saxonwold 2132, South Africa
Tel: (+27-11) 447 7172; Fax: (+27-11) 442 0728
E-mail: *res@sabisabi.com*
*www.sabisabi.com*

**Singita Private Game Reserve**
P.O. Box 23367, Claremont 7735, South Africa
Tel: (+27-21) 683 3424; Fax: (+27-21) 671 6776
E-mail: *reservations@singita.co.za*
*www.singita.com*

### KGALAGADI

**Kgalagadi Transfrontier Park (South Africa)**
South African National Parks
P.O. Box 787, Pretoria 0001, South Africa
Tel: (+27-12) 428 9111
Fax: (+27-12) 426 5500
E-mail: *reservations@sanparks.co.za*
*www.sanparks.org*

**Kgalagadi Transfrontier Park (Botswana)**
Parks & Reserves Reservations Office
P.O. Box 131, Gaborone, Botswana
Tel: +267-580 774; Fax: +267-580 775
E-mail: *parks.reservations.gaborone@gov.bw*
*www.botswana-tourism.gov.bw*

## NAMIBIA

### ETOSHA, DAMARALAND & KAOKOLAND

**Etosha National Park**
Namibia Wildlife Resorts Ltd
Private Bag 13267, Windhoek, Namibia
Tel: +264-61-285 7200; Fax 224 900
E-mail: *reservations@nwr.com.na*
*www.nwr.com.na*

**Wilderness Safaris – Damaraland, Ongava, Palmwag Rhino, Skeleton Coast Camps**
*www.wilderness-safaris.com*

## BOTSWANA

### OKAVANGO & MOREMI

**Moremi Game Reserve**
Parks & Reserves Reservations Office
P.O. Box 131, Gaborone, Botswana
Tel: +267-580 774; Fax: +267-580 775
E-mail: *parks.reservations.gaborone@gov.bw*
*www.botswana-tourism.gov.bw*

**Abu Camp Elephant Back Safaris**
Private Bag 332, Maun, Botswana
Tel: +267-686 1260; Fax 686 1005
E-mail: *ebs@info.bw*
*www.abucamp.com*

**Okavango Horse Safaris**
Private Bag 23, Maun, Botswana
Tel: +267-686 1671; Fax: +267-686 1672
E-mail: *safaris@okavangohorse.com*
*www.okavangohorse.com*

**Wilderness Safaris – Chitabe, Jao, Mombo, Xigera Camps**
*www.wilderness-safaris.com*

**Okavango Helicopters**
Private Bag 174, Maun, Botswana
Tel: +267-686 5797; Fax : +267-686 5798
E-mail: *okavangoheli@dynabyte.bw*

### CHOBE, LINYANTI & SAVUTI

**Desert & Delta Safaris – Chobe Game Lodge**
Private Bag 310, Maun, Botswana
Tel. Botswana: +267-686 1243
Tel. South Africa: (+27-11) 706 0861
E-mail: *reservations@desertdelta.com*
*www.desertdelta.com*

**Wilderness Safaris – Duma Tau, Kings Pool, Savuti Camps**
*www.wilderness-safaris.com*

## ZIMBABWE

### MANA POOLS & THE ZAMBEZI

**Mana Pools National Park**
Central Reservations Office Parks & Wildlife Management Authority
P.O. Box CY140, Causeway, Harare
Tel: +263-4-70 6077/8
E-mail: *natparks@africaonline.co.zw*
*www.zimparks.com*

**Wilderness Safaris – Chikwenya Camp**
*www.wilderness-safaris.com*

# ZAMBIA

## NORTH & SOUTH LUANGWA

**Zambia Wildlife Authority**
Private Bag 1, Chilanga, Zambia
Tel: +260-1-278 524/278 366
E-mail: *zawaorg@zamnet.zm*
*www.zawa.org.zm*

**The Bushcamp Company
– Bilimungwe, Kuyenda, Chamilandu,
Chindeni Camps & Mfuwe Lodge**
P.O. Box 91, Mfuwe, Zambia
Tel: +260-6-246 041; Fax: +44-8450-569 312
E-mail: *info@bushcampcompany.com*
*www.bushcampcompany.com*

**Remote Africa Safaris
– Tafika & Mwaleshi Camps,
Chikoko Trails**
P.O. Box 5, Mfuwe, Zambia
Tel: No phones – too remote!
E-mail: *tafika@remoteafrica.com*
*www.remoteafrica.com*

# TANZANIA

## NGORONGORO

**Ngorongoro Conservation Area
Authority**
P.O. Box 776, Arusha, Tanzania
Tel: +255-27-250 3339; Fax: 254 8752
*www.ngorongorocrater.org*

**Conservation Corporation
– Crater Lodge**
Private Bag X27, Benmore 2010, Sandown,
South Africa
Tel: (+27-11) 809 4441
E-mail: *safaris@ccafrica.com*
*www.ccafrica.com*

## SERENGETI

**Serengeti National Park**
Director General, Tanzania National Parks,
P.O. Box 3134, Arusha, Tanzania
Tel: +255-272-503 471
Fax: +255-272-508 216
E-mail: *info@tanzaniaparks.com*
*www.tanzaniaparks.com*

**Serengeti Balloon Safaris**
P.O. Box 12116, Arusha, Tanzania
Tel: +255-27-254 8967; Fax: 254 8997
E-mail: *info@balloonsafaris.com*
*www.balloonsafaris.com*

**Singita Grumeti Reserves – Sasakwa
& Faru Faru Lodge & Sabora Camp**
P.O. Box 23367, Claremont 7735, South Africa
Tel: (+27-21) 683 3424; Fax: 671 6776
E-mail: *reservations@singita.co.za*
*www.singita.com*

# KENYA

## MASAI MARA & LAKE NAKURU

**Karen Blixen Coffee Garden Cottages**
P.O. Box 163, Karen, Nairobi, Kenya
Tel: +254-20-88 2130/8; Fax: 88 2508
E-mail: *info@blixencoffeegarden.co.ke*
*www.blixencoffeegarden.co.ke*

**Lake Nakuru National Park**
Kenya Wildlife Service, P.O. Box 40241,
00100 Nairobi, Kenya
Tel: +254-20-60 0800;
Fax: +254-20-60 3792
E-mail: *kws@kws.org*
*www.kws.org*

**Newland & Tarlton Safaris**
11629 Quivas Circle, Westminster,
CO 80234, USA
Tel: +1-303-439 8426
E-mail: *info@newlandandtarlton.com*
*www.donyoungsafaris.com*

## AMBOSELI, TSAVO EAST & WEST

**Amboseli, Tsavo East & West National
Parks**
Kenya Wildlife Service, P.O. Box 40241,
00100 Nairobi, Kenya
Tel: +254-20-60 0800; Fax: 60 3792
E-mail: *kws@kws.org*
*www.kws.org*

# RWANDA & UGANDA

**Mgahinga Gorilla & Bwindi
Impenetrable National Parks**
Uganda Wildlife Authority
P.O. Box 3530, Kampala, Uganda
Tel: +256-41-355 000; Fax: +256-41-346 291
E-mail: *uwa@uwa.or.ug*
*www.uwa.or.ug*

**Primate Safaris**
Avenue de la Paix 98,
BP 4158, Kigali, Rwanda
Tel: +250-501 934/503 428
E-mail: *office@primatesafaris-rwanda.com*
*www.primatesafaris-rwanda.com*

**Parc National des Volcans**
The Rwanda Tourism Board
P.O. Box 905, Kigali, Rwanda
Tel: +250-576 514; Fax +250-576 515
E-mail: *reservation@rwandatourism.com*
*www.rwandatourism.com*

# CONSERVATION
*(for enquiries and donations)*

**Frankfurt Zoological Society (Africa)**
P.O. Box 14935, Arusha, Tanzania
Tel: +255-28-262 1506;
Fax: +255-28-262 1537
E-mail: *info@fzs.org*
*www.fzs.org*

**South African National Parks
Veterinary Wildlife Services**
SANParks, P.O. Box 787, Pretoria 0001
Tel: (+27-12) 426 5000
E-mail: *enquiries@sanparks.org*
*www.sanparks.org*

**Game Capture Unit, Scientific Services
Ministry of Environment & Tourism**
Private Bag 13306, Windhoek, Namibia
Tel: +264-61-284 2543;
Fax: +264-61-260 062
E-mail: *gamecap@iafrica.com.na*

Reprinted in 2019

This edition published in 2016 by
John Beaufoy Publishing Ltd
11 Blenheim Court, 316 Woodstock Road, Oxford OX2 7NS, England
www.johnbeaufoy.com

Design concept: Peter and Beverly Pickford
Design: Alessandro Bonora
Editor: Mary Duncan
Illustrations: Alessandro Bonora
Reproduction by Resolution Colour (Pty) Ltd, Cape Town
Printed and bound in Malaysia by Times Offset (M) Sdn. Bhd.

ISBN 978-1-909612-87-7

# ACKNOWLEDGEMENTS

The authors would like to express their thanks to all those individuals, governments
and wildlife departments whose contributions made this journey and book possible.
In addition, thanks to Brian Graham for allowing the use of the photographs of the
Burton/Taylor wedding (page 132).

The publisher acknowledges the use of extracts from:
• *Flaubert's Parrot* by Julian Barnes, published by Jonathan Cape.
  © Julian Barnes 1983.
• *Green Hills of Africa* by Ernest Hemingway, published by Jonathan Cape.
  Reprinted by permission of The Random House Group Ltd.